How to Understand the Creed

Jean-Noël Bezançon, Jean-Marie Onfray
and Philippe Ferlay

How to Understand
the Creed

SCM PRESS LTD

Translated by John Bowden from the French
Pour Dire le Credo
published 1987 by Les Editions du Cerf
29 bd Latour-Maubourg, Paris

© Les Editions du Cerf 1987

Translation © John Bowden 1987

Nihil obstat: Father Anton Cowan
Censor

Imprimitur: Rt. Rev. John Crowley, VG
Bishop in Central London
Westminster, 14 June 1987

The Nihil obstat *and* Imprimatur *are a declaration
that a book or pamphlet is considered to be free from
doctrinal or moral error. It is not implied that those who
have granted the* Nihil obstat *and* Imprimatur *agree
with the contents, opinions or statements expressed.*

British Library Cataloguing in Publication Data
Bezancon, Jean-Noel
How to understand the creed.
1. Apostles' Creed
I. Title   II. Onfray, Jean-Marie
III. Ferlay, Philippe   IV. Pour dire le
credo. *English*
238'.11   BT993.2

ISBN 0–334–02038–7

First published in English 1987
by SCM Press Ltd, 26–30 Tottenham Road, London N1

Typeset at The Spartan Press Ltd, Lymington, Hants
and printed in Great Britain by
Richard Clay (The Chaucer Press) Ltd, Bungay, Suffolk

Contents

References in italics are to the material in boxes

The Nicene Creed

We believe in one God,
   the Father, the Almighty,
   maker of heaven and earth,
   of all that is, seen and unseen.

We believe in one Lord, Jesus Christ,
   the only Son of God,
   eternally begotten of the Father,
   God from God, Light from Light,
   true God from true God,
   begotten, not made,
   of one Being with the Father.
   Through him all things were made.
For us men and for our salvation
   he came down from heaven:
by the power of the Holy Spirit
   he became incarnate from the Virgin Mary,
   and was made man.
For our sake he was crucified under Pontius Pilate;
   he suffered death and was buried.
   On the third day he rose again
     in accordance with the scriptures;
   he ascended into heaven
     and is seated at the right hand of the Father.
He will come again in glory to judge the living and the
   dead,
   and his kingdom will have no end.

We believe in the Holy Spirit, the Lord, the giver of life,
   who proceeds from the Father and the Son.
   With the Father and the Son he is worshipped and
     glorified.
   He has spoken through the Prophets.
   We believe in one holy catholic and apostolic Church.
   We acknowledge one baptism for the forgiveness of sins.
   We look for the resurrection of the dead,
     and the life of the world to come. Amen.

Our Baptismal Creed

The church says what is has done

We have considerable difficulty in seeing the Church for what it really is: the community which proclaims the gospel, the good news of Christ, so that men and women can be happy; the community which enables men and women to live by the sacraments that Christ has given to it, including, particularly and from the very beginning, the most beautiful sacrament of baptism. That is how the Church exists, i.e. the Church as the community of those who accept the love of the Father and risk the adventure of living his life:

> 'Go therefore and make disciples of all nations, baptizing them' (Matt. 28.19).

We often attach more importance to the words of the Church (statements by the Pope, declarations by our bishops) than to its actions, and these words give us the impression that the Church is an institution for making pronouncements, a very worthy old lady who talks a good deal. Certainly the Church talks, and it has to, to tell men and women once again about the beauty of the teaching of Jesus and to help them towards being converted in their hearts.

But in its profound truth the Church first acts, and it is by reflecting on this action that it speaks and discovers what it has first done. In this way it verifies the truth of its action and explains its value.

The Church performs baptisms, performs this mysterious action which allows a person to know that he or she is loved by the Father and united to Jesus, thus becoming a witness to the universal love of the Father through the power of the Spirit of Jesus. We all need constantly to rediscover the beauty and the importance of the baptism that we have received.

And it is in close connection with this act of baptism that the Church presents the creed, so that those who have been baptized may recognize together the treasure in which they share, without any merits on their part. We must always repeat to ourselves Paul's saying: 'For by grace you have been saved; and this is not your own doing, it is the gift of God' (Eph. 2.8). So the creed is a kind of road map which indicates the beauties of this new world to whose shores the sacrament of baptism has brought us. The confession of faith is an introduction to wonder and the prayer of thanksgiving.

A God who raises questions

If we are to study and understand the creed, it is vital for us not to forget the time of our own baptisms, when the priest or the deacon summed up the faith of the Church in the form of three questions: 'Do you believe in the Father? Do you believe in Jesus Christ? Do you believe in the Holy Spirit?

In the ancient baptismal liturgy, each time the candidate replied, 'Yes, I believe', he or she was immersed in running water.

This threefold question asked by the Church is inseparable from the questions which Jesus asked of those men and women whom he met in his earthly life: 'Who do you think that I am?' Our God asks questions.

God comes to meet humankind. He does not come simply to exhibit or show himself, boasting of his beauty. He indicates a way and invites us to follow it with him: 'Come, follow me.' It is as we take this way that we shall discover the beauties of the country through which we go. But God is honest, and first of all he says: 'Do you want to follow me? Who am I to you?'

We say 'Yes' to love

The text of the creed that we shall be reading is therefore inseparable from a living commitment, from a reply which involves us. The creed is not a manual, an instruction book which we are given along with a vehicle, which we put in the glove compartment and hope to use as little as possible.

Its text must first of all be inscribed on our hearts, as a profound certainty which may perhaps be spelt out only rarely, at times of extreme importance, but which will inspire our everyday action. Our brothers in the early churches never had any text of the creed to refer to: they had heard it, received it from their forebears, and had to learn it before handing it on in their turn. And many died a martyr death to communicate its whole truth.

So studying the creed is not primarily a matter of instructing oneself, enriching one's mind, but of bearing witness: it is a matter of bearing witness, if need be at the cost of one's life, that the love of God is true, that he brings life, that he renews life and hope, that he makes people happy.

I or we?

With all the passion of a convert, Maurice Clavel was fond of saying: 'I only exist if God says "Thou" to me.' And he was right in the sense that God does not love men and women indiscriminately, but loves each individual, suggesting to each man and each women, in the depths of their hearts, the adventure of life with him and of shared love.

In this sense the creed has a personal root, and today I must say 'I believe' as a statement which commits me most deeply.

However, the Second Vatican Council reminds us that it was not the will of God to call human beings independently of one another, but to bring them together in a single family, the divine model for which is trinitarian communion.

In this sense we never say the creed by ourselves, and even someone who whispers it in the silence of his or her room finds a place in the communion of faith of a Church which has long existed in the past and which far transcends us all.

Here, as in many spheres, truth is to be found in an equilibrium, not in a choice which excludes every other possibility. When we say the creed, we say it both for ourselves and also as the Church.

So with this book, in close communion with our Church, let us go on to study and try to understand the creed.

The Church has gone before us in time and has handed down the creed to us, that Church in which we have been born or which we rejoined when we were grown up. It goes back to the time of the apostles, the companions of Jesus; the time of those who worked out the confession of faith that we shall be studying step by step. And we shall be studying the creed in close communion with those men and women who died martyr deaths to bear witness to the beauty and the truth of the faith which they professed.

This Church which surrounds us is catholic in the strict sense, in other words, is extended throughout the world. All cultures are expressed in it, all the riches of humankind appear in it, and there are no lack of martyrs in it, known or unknown.

Paul's confessions of faith

It is important that we may note the hint of a creed in Paul, the first Christian writer. A creed is already taking shape, and soon it will develop further, in the face of threats and struggles.

The most explicit sketch is to be found towards the end of the first letter to the Christians of Corinth:

> Now I would remind you, brethren, in what terms I preached to you the gospel, which you received, in which you stand, by which you are saved, if you hold it fast – unless you believed in vain. For I delivered to you as of first importance what I also received, that Christ died for our sins in accordance with the scriptures, that he was buried, that he was raised on the third day in accordance with the scriptures, and that he appeared to Cephas (Peter), then to the twelve. Then he appeared to more than five hundred brethren at one time, most of whom are still alive, though some have fallen asleep. Then he appeared to James, then to all the apostles. Last of all, as to one untimely born, he appeared also to me . . . (I Cor. 15.1–8).

This is a short formula which puts all the stress on Christ's death and resurrection. If we are looking for a formula which is closer to the creed as we now have it, why not keep the end of another epistle, which we often hear as an introduction to the eucharist or as a closing prayer:

> The grace of the Lord Jesus Christ and the love of God and the fellowship of the Holy Spirit be with you all (II Cor. 13.14).

St Paul preaching in Athens. Engraving by Bellanger, 1749. Photo Roger-Viollet

From the Gospel to the Creed

Without thinking very hard, one could say: since the creed exists, let's read it; let's see what it contains. But if we were to start like that it would be very surprising if someone who was disturbed or who wanted to contradict did not get up and say, 'Why do we need a creed anyway?' 'Do we need a creed, let alone several creeds? Isn't the creed like ivy growing round a tree and drawing off its sap, which has covered over the real branch of the message of the gospel, or like a chapel added at a later stage which disturbs the harmony of a romanesque church?'

So before studying the creed, we need to know why it exists in the first place.

Even if the Gospels were enough . . .

Why are the four Gospels not enough to express the faith of the disciples of Jesus? These four books contain the essentials of what we need to know about the existence of Jesus Christ, Son of God, Saviour. There we have his teaching, in various forms all of which are alive. And every catechist has experienced the impact of even one page of the gospel on a group of attentive children.

But the formula which we have just used, 'Jesus Christ, Son of God, Saviour', the Greek initials of which are the letters which spell Ichthus, fish, does not appear in any of the Gospels, and already represents a theological construction developed from the Gospel narratives. That should be enough to explain that a simple reading of the four books, the one gospel in four forms, as Irenaeus of Lyons put it at the end of the second century, is not enough to express the faith of Christians. The faith of Christians is simple, and can be summed up in a few striking and vivid phrases, but we do not find these particular indispensable phrases in the pages of our Gospels.

Beyond question there is a harmony between the four Gospels, and each of them tells us of an extraordinary man who arose in the midst of history to give it an absolute sense, a man who has to be recognized as a unique Saviour if we are to express his impact on human history.

But as soon as we read the Gospels, either one after the other or in parallel (in a synopsis), we find numerous differences, not to say contradictions. There are differences in the narrative itself: how many years did the public ministry of Jesus last, and did he make just one journey to Jerusalem, the city where he was to be crucified and rise again, or more? It is only in their presentation of the trial and death of Jesus that the Gospels agree. We find numerous important differences when it comes to the resurrection and the encounters of the Risen Jesus with his community.

And then, each of the evangelists has his own theology: he presents a particular portrait, with vivid contrasts, of this Jesus of whom he speaks. Granted we must not exaggerate the differences, but it would be dishonest to pass over them in silence, to develop the four Gospels into a single one, something in which the Church has never succeeded.

It seems that by themselves the four books of the Gospel would never be enough either to express or to structure the faith in order to unite in the same proclamation those men and women who confess their allegiance to Jesus.

The example and witness of Paul

Paul, converted before Damascus, is the first Christian author. And he made his mark on Christian literature with unparalleled force. Fourteen of his letters found a place in the canon of our scriptures, whereas only five works of John, the beloved disciple, are included in our New Testament.

When Paul wrote to the Christians of Thessalonica, in Greece, probably about 51, none of the Gospels had been composed in the forms with which we are familiar, even if collections of sayings were already in circulation among the communities. And precisely in order to express the faith, to proclaim it joyfully, Paul was obliged to engage in theology; he developed confessions of faith, the beginnings of a creed (see the box on page 63). He did not do this for pleasure, but because he needed to express the significance of the person and the life of Christ. He wanted to speak of this mystery which for him – as we should note – is not the mystery of God in his inaccessible greatness, but that of the love of God for us, of his plan of salvation realized in Christ, of that so great love (Eph. 2.4), with which the Father loves humankind, manifesting it in the death and resurrection of the Son and the gift of the Spirit.

When Paul speaks of scripture he is referring to the Old Testament. And when, like Matthew, he shows that Jesus did everything according to the scriptures, it is to demonstrate the continuity and the coherence of this whole divine plan which has been fulfilled in Christ, and which manifests itself before him through the existence of the churches.

The faith which love seeks to understand

So it is in the succession of Paul and all the first communities that we require a creed and that we still present the confession of faith in this form. We do not do it for the pleasure of speculating or to demonstrate our intelligence, but for three inseparable reasons:

1. We want to understand better what we believe, to look at it in a better light and to wonder at it even more. We must never forget that the prime motive power behind theological work is wonder at the love with which we are loved.

2. We have to proclaim the good news, the Gospel, to all those who do not yet know it. Those who proclaim the faith must utter the mystery, even if they retain considerable liberty in the way in which they present it. The creed must not be a strait-jacket, but a guide. And it is primarily a guide to missionary preaching. It is in this spirit that it is presented and commented on by all those who want to become Christians and go in 'the Way'.

3. Finally, the creed is necessary to unite in a single body the different churches of God spread over the surface of the world. Granted, each church has its own way of speaking and even more its own way of living. Paul saw this clearly in the different communities of the Mediterranean basin which he founded or encountered. We too are well aware of it now, since the Second Vatican Council has freed us from too rigid a uniformity and has encouraged a greater diversity of cultural expressions of the one faith. But the more the diversity is manifested, the more the one creed must be the tie which holds together the sheaf and keeps the various communities as a single family, to use another phrase from Irenaeus, himself a witness to this diversity and this profound unity, since he came from Asia Minor and ended up preaching in Lyons, in France.

So the creed is necessary for the faith of the churches, as the living faith of each baptized Christian.

A holy bishop.
Romanesque fresco

A confession of faith by Irenaeus of Lyons

Here is the rule of our faith, the foundation of the building and that which gives steadfastness to our conduct:

God the Father, uncreated, who is not contained, invisible, one God, the creator of the universe; that is the very first article of our faith. And the second article is:

The Word of God, the Son of God, Christ Jesus our Lord, who appeared to the prophets after the manner of their prophecy and the state of the economies of the Father; by whom all things were made; who moreover at the end of time, to recapitulate all things, was made man among humankind, visible and palpable, to destroy death, bring forth life and achieve communion between God and man.

And as the third article:

The Holy Spirit by whom the prophets prophesied and the Fathers have learned the things of God, and the righteous have been guided in the way of righteousness and who, at the end of time, has been poured forth in a new way on our humanity to renew humankind over all the earth in the face of God.

Demonstration of the Apostolic Preaching, no. 6.

Father and Son in the Spirit

There is no denying the trinitarian structure of the creed; it is based on the threefold question put to those being baptized. The mystery of the Trinity must still be understood as a living and life-giving reality, and not just as a theoretical framework, a convenient catalogue of the essential truths of our faith.

Ministry of the Son and ministry of the Spirit

We shall not be talking of the Father immediately. It is indeed true that everything comes from him and returns to him, but it is from the actions of the Son and the life-giving presence of the Spirit in human hearts that we know him better and that we discover the ways which lead to his more intimate character.

The first part of the work of salvation, of this mystery of which Paul speaks, devised by the Father in his immense love, extends from the act of creation to the resurrection of Jesus. He acted so that this Son should come, in order to make possible his incarnation. One cannot make the incarnation nothing more than a remedy for sin, as if the Father *invented* the incarnation in a catastrophe in order to resolve the problem raised by an unforeseen mistake. Paul says, in an infinitely wide perspective:

> The Father chose us in Christ before the foundation of the world, that we should be holy and blameless before him. He destined us in love (Eph. 1.4). (See chapter 12, page 63.)

And throughout this immense period the Spirit acted as a minister for the Son; the Spirit participated in the Father's plan so that the incarnation should take place and succeed. He is the Creator Spirit, who prepares all things with a view to the incarnation of the Beloved Son: he prepares for the coming into being of the vastness of humanity. He shaped the people of Israel, among whom was born 'he who should come'. And finally, he came upon Mary, leading her to hail the surprising news that she was to give birth to the Saviour. It was the Spirit who accompanied Jesus through his human life, and who brought him to his cross and resurrection.

From the joyful dawn of the resurrection the Son is glorified with the Father and with him sends the Spirit. As he has benefited from the ministry of the Spirit, so now he puts himself at the service of the Spirit, so that his cross and resurrection can bear their fruit, not only in the man Jesus but in the hearts of all men and women throughout the world.

We live in the time of the Spirit

As we study the creed today we should never forget that we are living in the time of the activity of the Spirit.

The work of the Spirit is immense, yet infinitely varied, and respects the mystery of individuals. It is for each man and woman to welcome the love of the Spirit, to allow himself or herself to be conformed to Christ by this love, so as to become in him a son or daughter of the Father and be able to say with Paul: 'It is no longer I who live, but Christ who lives in me' (Gal. 2.20).

This is the time in which we live, this time which takes place in us, even if we are too little aware of the fact. And when we say or study the creed, it is not primarily to formulate our faith in a rationally satisfying way but to adapt ourselves to this action of the Spirit which transforms us and unites us to the spiritual adventure of Christ. It is doubtless for this reason that in the creed we speak above all of Christ and of his work, even if we are in the time of the Spirit. And it is not only because we know that better, that we have more to say about it, but also because the spiritual adventure of Christ is the model for our own adventure. And the Spirit of the holy poverty of God readily accepts being moved in to the background in this way and often being forgotten: provided that the work of salvation goes forward and is accomplished.

The Spirit builds up the Body of Christ

The previous paragraph might have given the misleading impression that the Spirit acts only with human hearts, that it is interested only in human individuals, and transforms only each person's conscience, conforming it to Christ.

At the same time as it transforms hearts, the Spirit builds up the Church, the body of Christ.

Augustine was fond of preaching that 'the true Christ is him and us'. And if we study the creed, if we look at it in order to proclaim it together, in particular when we celebrate the eucharist, it is because we know that this proclamation is useful, and that it contributes towards building up the Church as the Father has wanted from all eternity. It is necessary for the Church to build itself up in the service of the world so that one day Christ can present it to the Father, 'holy and pure, like a bride adorned for her husband' (Eph. 5.27).

Until this hour has come, the great work of salvation goes on, and we would be wrong to believe that the essentials have been completed and that Christian life for individuals and the Church simply consists in waiting. We must work on until the evening, with courage and confidence. 'Woe is me if I do not preach the gospel,' exclaimed Paul. Too many places remain empty around the Father's table. And we also study the creed to become aware once again of our missionary responsibility.

For the glory of the Father, who is the life of humankind

At the heart of our faith is the conviction that two things are not opposed but come together in the mysterious will of the Father: God does not take pleasure in seeing humanity destroy itself, but rejoices at its true joy. Irenaeus gave marvellous expression to this:

> The glory of God is living humanity
> but the life of humanity is to see God.

And the Son, like the Spirit, opens himself and spends himself in the service of the Father. It is from him that Son and Spirit come, it is him that they love with all their strength, it is the service of his glory which gives meaning to their eternal existences. Jesus was fond of saying, as a definition of his life as a human being and as the Son: 'I love the Father, and I always do what is pleasing to him' (John 8.29).

So the proclamation of our whole creed is directed towards the Father. It is important to indicate at the beginning of our study the degree to which if the Father is the source of the whole mystery of salvation he is also its goal, the one in whom all is fulfilled. Because we shall never cease from wondering at the love with which he fills us and which is his most intimate being (see the end of Part Three).

A confession of faith by our brothers of the Reformation

I believe that God has created me and all other creatures. He has given me my body with its members and my spirit with its faculties, and he keeps them in being. Each day he gives me abundant food, clothing, a home and all things necessary to support this life. He protects me from all dangers, preserves me and delivers me from all evil; all this without my being worthy of it, through his sheer goodness and fatherly mercy.

This is what I firmly believe.

I believe that Jesus Christ, true God and true man, is my Lord. He has redeemed me, lost and condemned though I am, by delivering me from sin, from death and the power of the Evil One, not at the price of gold and silver, but by his suffering and by his innocent death, so that I may belong to him for ever and live a new life like him who, risen from the dead, lives and reigns eternally.

This is what I firmly believe.

I believe that the Holy Spirit calls me by the gospel, illuminates me by his gifts and sanctifies me; that he keeps me in the unity of the true faith, in the Church which he brings together day by day. He, too, it is who fully forgives me my sins, as he does those of all believers. It is he who on the

Luther, by Lucas Cranach. Munich.
Photo Roger-Viollet

last day will raise me with all the dead and give me life eternal in Jesus Christ.

This is what I firmly believe.

Confession of faith of the Reformed Church of France based on Martin Luther.

Our Creeds in History

Before we set out to study our creed, it is worth saying a few words about the origin of the texts that we have, texts that we often proclaim without really understanding to what degree they place us in the long tradition of Christian history.

The truth of a legend

The formulation of our creeds was crystallized in the context of the celebration of baptism. The creed always originates in the threefold question asked at baptism:

> Do you believe in the Father, the source of all things?
> Do you believe in his Son Jesus, who became man to save us?
> Do you believe in the Holy Spirit, who gives life to the Church?

What we call the 'Apostles' Creed' or the *little* creed is an ancient profession of faith from the community in Rome. It is very old, and is sometimes said to have a very venerable origin: it has been claimed that it was produced by the apostles themselves in Jerusalem before they separated and set off on their world-wide mission. People have even gone so far as to attribute particular clauses to particular apostles, associating these clauses with personal characteristics or teachings of individual apostles. In the abbey of Hauterive in Switzerland you can see stalls in which each of the twelve apostles is holding in his hand a banner proclaiming the phrase from the creed which goes back to him.

This is a legend, but like all legends, it contains its due degree of teaching. Even if the apostles had other things to do than gather round a table to work out a creed with twelve articles, the legend makes us understand that the faith which we proclaim is still that of the companions of Christ Jesus. It is from them that we receive everything: proper knowledge of the personal mystery of Jesus, his action on behalf of humanity and the marvellous plan of the Father for his glory and our happiness, a plan realized in the power of the Spirit by the ministry of the Church.

We rarely say this creed of the apostles which tends, rather, to find a place in personal prayer; many people have forgotten the exact text. But let us remember how close it is to the faith of the apostles.

By imperial decree

When the three hundred bishops, almost all from the East, who had responded to the summons of the emperor Constantine in spring 325, entered the gilded portals of the imperial palace at Nicaea, near the shores of the Black Sea, many people thought that the end of time was near. The praetorian guard paid their respects to these men who were living memorials of a violent persecution. They included old Paphnutius, one of whose eyes had been plucked out by the imperial torturers, and the young bishops kissed the hollow socket with deep emotion. Was this not the triumph of Christ?

Without too much difficulty they agreed on a condemnation of the priest Arius of Alexandria, who had failed to do justice to Christ by presenting him as being inferior to the Father. But things deteriorated when the emperor, who was not even baptized, compelled the bishops to agree on a text expressing a common confession of faith. He did not do things by halves, since he punished with exile those who refused to sign the text. Each local church had its own text for confessing the faith, which was used for catechesis preparatory to baptism, but they dreaded the uniformity that a single text would bring.

Finally, making the most of a bad job, the bishops adopted as a basic text the confession of faith of the church of Caesarea in Palestine, presented by its bishop Eusebius, the famous historian of the first centuries of the Church. The fathers studied the text and inserted into it the famous 'consubstantial', of the same nature (*homoousios*), which was to prove so difficult to impose during subsequent decades. It took all the courage of Athanasius of Alexandria to defend it against the opposition. The Nicene creed was born, and we should find it moving to recite the creed each Sunday, since it comes to us across the ages, from distant Asia Minor where the faith first came to be born.

Some very curious bishops

In 381 a local Council brought together a certain number of bishops from the area in Constantinople. Basil of Caesarea had died two years earlier,

but his shadow lay over the work of the Council, inspired by his friend Gregory of Nazianzus. It was concerned to make more precise that part of the confession of faith which relates to the Holy Spirit, since dissident movements challenged the divinity of the Spirit and therefore his action in the mystery of salvation.

So the bishops took the risk of slightly amplifying the text of Nicaea and developing the confession of faith by including in it the Holy Spirit, who is 'the Lord and giver of life'. This is the text which we still have and which will serve as our guide; apart, that is, from the famous insertion about the Spirit who proceeds from the Father 'and the Son' (*Filioque*), which does not figure in the primitive text and the addition of which by the West provoked the indignation of our Eastern brothers.

For the bishops present at Constantinople made an affirmation of major importance: we are modifying the text of Nicaea because we think that this modification is indispensable, but it should be noted that it will not be possible to do such a thing after us! In the following century, in 451, when a great assembly of bishops met at Chalcedon on the banks of the Bosphorus, the text of Nicaea was proclaimed in its retouched

A Council. Based on a tenth-century miniature. Photo Roger-Viollet

11

version and recognized as the confession of faith of all the churches.

Even if everyday Christian life sometimes seems to turn the creed the opposite way round, in the sense that we prefer to begin from the mystery of Christ and the action of the Spirit in the Church and get back to the Father, the goal of all things, it is in fidelity to the heritage of the Church that we shall now be studying and reading the creed together.

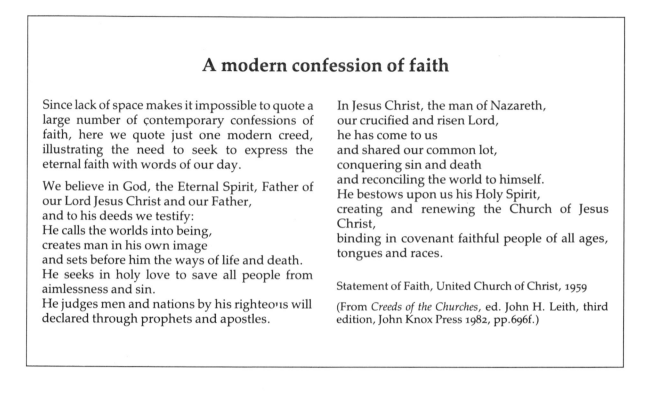

A modern confession of faith

Since lack of space makes it impossible to quote a large number of contemporary confessions of faith, here we quote just one modern creed, illustrating the need to seek to express the eternal faith with words of our day.

We believe in God, the Eternal Spirit, Father of our Lord Jesus Christ and our Father,
and to his deeds we testify:
He calls the worlds into being,
creates man in his own image
and sets before him the ways of life and death.
He seeks in holy love to save all people from aimlessness and sin.
He judges men and nations by his righteous will declared through prophets and apostles.

In Jesus Christ, the man of Nazareth,
our crucified and risen Lord,
he has come to us
and shared our common lot,
conquering sin and death
and reconciling the world to himself.
He bestows upon us his Holy Spirit,
creating and renewing the Church of Jesus Christ,
binding in covenant faithful people of all ages, tongues and races.

Statement of Faith, United Church of Christ, 1959

(From *Creeds of the Churches*, ed. John H. Leith, third edition, John Knox Press 1982, pp.696f.)

PART ONE

1   I Believe in One God

Is reason enough?

We should not hesitate to start from what human intelligence can discover of its own accord; that is not to scorn the newness of the faith but to root it in its true origin: the God who created human kind is the saviour in his Son.

Now reason discovers the oneness of God: it could not cope with a number of gods. To affirm any kind of pantheon of deities is inevitably to subordinate these gods to one another and little by little to move towards the affirmation of a super-God. Greek philosophy developed in this direction, and many religions, which began with a numerous pantheon in which each deity had his particular function, developed in the direction of a vague monotheism. That happened with the affirmation of the sun as the one god, which spread throughout the Roman empire in the time of Constantine.

The affirmation of faith in the framework of the covenant

We would neglect the human dimensions of the Bible if we were to say that things were quite different for Israel. Some ancient psalms retain traces of this assembly of gods, or even mention the gods of the nations, to say that they are subject to the God of Israel. It is only in the time of Second Isaiah, towards the sixth century, i.e. relatively late, that these gods will be said categorically to be nothing.

For biblical and Christian monotheism does not have its origins in philosophical reflection but in the specific and living reality of the covenant. The one God is the God who made a covenant with Israel on Sinai, so that this people should become his privileged witness to the nations.

And we Christians should base our faith in God on the new covenant made between God and the world by Jesus. We shall be constantly repeating the close connection between creed and baptism. It is always painful to hear someone asked about his or her faith as a Christian replying, 'I believe that there is a good God!' We must keep more closely to the God who made a covenant with men and women in Christ.

I am a jealous God

This basic character of the covenant is presented, from the divine point of view, by what the texts call his jealousy. There can be no question of that petty feeling which we often have and which makes us take umbrage at the success of others. The term 'divine jealousy' is an imaginative way of expressing the passion that God has for his people, the seriousness with which he takes the covenant.

God is jealous, because he does not just pretend to love. When we say the creed, we are not make cold statements. We are affirming the reality of 'God for us'. And no one should claim that the preaching of the gospel has freed us from this jealousy of the God of Israel. Jesus is the servant of this Father and he wants our life no longer to be just for ourselves (II Cor. 5.15).

The service of the one God

'The one before whom I stand is the living God,' the prophet Elijah proudly proclaimed when confronted with the vanity of the baals, the false gods. We should understand the degree to which the proclamation of the creed commits us to the same certainty. The one of whom we speak, the one whom we name, is the living God who gives us life. And if we study the creed, not as an ancient document, but as believers, we agree to live for this God.

It is as the Living One that our God is the one God. His oneness is that of a burning love which cannot be quenched or parcelled out. The proclamation of the creed of Christians is at the service of the testimony given to the living God.

Romanesque fresco from Taüll, Spain, 1123. Detail of the apse. Photo private collection

16

Christian monotheism and Asian polytheism

Asia is organized into two great complexes situated one on either side of the Himalayas: one, to the south-south-east, under Indian influence and the other, to the north-north-east, under Chinese influence, but each allowing a degree of racial, cultural and religious pluralism.

It is useful to begin our enquiry with Hinduism, the main religion of India.

Hinduism is a religion without dogmas and without a central authority. Everyone can choose, from the immense treasury of its sacred scriptures and local and family traditions, the way which allows him or her finally to escape this illusory world to become lost in the supreme reality, Brahman. These ways differ, but the most popular is that of devotion to one of the traditional deities, Brahma, Shiva, Vishnu, or one or other of their numerous incarnations (avatars), like Rama, Krishna or even their feminine counterparts (shaktis). What is the relationship between these deities and Brahman? From what the Hindus tell us these are simply the different names of the one supreme God. But is he personal or impersonal? That is a problem for Westerners, but there is no indication that it is a problem for Indians.

Buddhism was born in India out of the same concern as that of Hinduism, namely to free human beings from suffering, liberating them from the infinite cycle of rebirth. The method differs only at certain points, but these are important. To achieve salvation the Buddhist must not count on the help of any deity, since all are powerless, but only on his personal effort at purification by asceticism, meditation and knowledge.

Although it has disappeared from India almost completely, Buddhism has spread throughout the Far East. Even within India it had diversified into several schools. This phenomenon of evolution has been further accentuated by the demands of the cultures that it has encountered along its way. But among all these shifts it is important to stress what makes Buddhism a true religion of salvation. For while qualified bonzes see the Buddha only as a master who opens up the way of liberation, there is no disputing the fact that for many disciples the Buddhas and Boddhisatvas are beings belonging to a superior world, to whom one can pray in the distresses of life in the present, and in order to acquire happiness in a world to come.

In China it is customary to say that there are three religions: Confucianism, Taoism and Buddhism. The formula is simple, but inadequate.

Confucianism, which has also left its stamp on part of Japan, Korea and Vietnam, is above all a way of living in conformity with a personal, family, social and political ethic. But up to the 1911 revolution this religion always incorporated the cult of Heaven in which it has been possible to see, above all at its beginnings, a hint of monotheism. Only a hint, since beside Heaven, many celestial and terrestrial spirits have always received their share of homage and prayer. Moreover, for a long time scholarly Confucians have done away with this religious aspect of Heaven at the expense of cosmological speculations. However, ordinary people have not necessarily followed the scholars, and until recent times, for many Chinese the venerable Father of Heaven was equivalent to the God of the Christians.

With Confucianism, Taoism is the other profound aspect of China. In the earliest works which try to define it, it appears both as a metaphysical quest and a life-style in full har-

→

mony with nature. The Tao is present as a hidden power, outside our intelligence, situated beyond the universe but immanent or present to each of the ten thousand beings which make it up, albeit in futility. An expert on China has called this an evolution towards pantheism.

But Taoism is also a popular religion bearing witness to a passionate quest for immortality, waning in continental China but alive in Taiwan or Hong Kong. In this form it has kept or recovered innumerable ancient deities often specific to one or other area. Some observers see this as an excessive form of polytheism. But others see here only a fervent veneration of more or less efficacious local patron saints.

We should not draw simple conclusions from all this. When one begins to listen to the religions of Asia it is impossible to say just one thing about them. We quite often encounter attitudes which from a Western perspective might appear atheistic, pantheistic or polytheistic. But when one tries to get to the heart of the matter, one also discovers an authentic spiritual quest and even serious points of contact which should allow Christian monotheism to enter into fruitful dialogue with them.

Fr Antoine Carret

2   The Church Believes in the Father of Jesus

When the Church asks questions at the moment of administering baptism it does not simply say 'Do you believe in God?' It asks, 'Do you believe in God, the Father Almighty?' Thus naming God as Father is an essential part of the confession of faith.

The true Father of Jesus

Again we must understand what kind of fatherhood this is. It is wrong to suppose that Israel was ignorant of the mystery of the fatherhood of God: God was proclaimed the Father of the people, of the king, and he was considered as being in a special way the Father of the Messiah who was to come. When Jesus presents himself as Son of the Father he is not making some staggering affirmation (see Part II, chapter 10, pages 50ff.).

What changes everything is the way in which Jesus makes this affirmation: God is his Father in a unique way, he is his Abba. Jesus knows him and lives in perfect intimacy with him, in a unique knowledge and a total sharing of his plan of love. Jesus always makes a distinction. He says 'My Father and your Father' (John 20.17), and when he teaches how sons should pray, he does not say, 'Let us pray together', but 'When you pray, say . . .'

Only the gift of the Spirit, beyond the experience of Easter, will allow us to enter into communion with Jesus as sons. Paul had a vivid awareness of this: 'No one can say Abba, Father, save by the Holy Spirit' (Rom. 8.15; Gal. 4.6).

Loved with the same love

However, once this adoption has been realized, it is sincere and without any evasions on the part of God. The Father offers us, each man and each woman, the same love that he offers to his only Son. The word adoption stresses God's absolute freedom; there is nothing unreal in his action.

And this is perhaps the essential affirmation of faith, that which, definitively, brings us together to proclaim this creed. We are loved by the Father with the same love that he bears his only Son, the love with which we see him love Jesus. The saying 'You are my well-beloved child, in whom I am well pleased' (Mark 1.11; Luke 3.22) is strictly true for each one of us, male or female.

It is on this certainty that the adventure of faith is based and becomes a peaceful progress towards encountering a love which comes first and is always undeserved. It is the truth of the word said by God himself, who attacks my sin and destroys it. Is not absolute sin the definitive refusal to be involved at this point?

The structure of Christian prayer

From earliest antiquity Christian prayer has structured itself on this certainty. Jesus is worthy of our prayers, he is Lord. And yet, in the vast majority of cases, we do not pray to him but with him, aware of sharing in his experience as Son, in the Spirit.

Even if the creed is not directly a prayer, it readily finds a place in liturgical prayer, in particular on Sundays and festivals. Those who have recognized in Christ the mystery of the Fatherhood of God, who have affirmed it as the basis of their faith – I believe in God, the Father Almighty – will address him at the climax of their celebration with the words of Jesus. They will dare to do so because of the Lord's command and even more so because of the certainty that the Spirit of Jesus is within them.

'The Word was with God'. Detail of the polyptych of St Peter by Meister Bertram. fourteenth century, Hamburg. Photo private collection

Divine Unity and Trinity

Although the Christian affirmation of God comes into being in a context of the strictest monotheism and never rejects that monotheism, it recognizes Jesus as Lord, to whom prayers are to be offered and who is himself Saviour. Thus it provides at least the roots of a possible dualism between the action of the invisible God and that of Jesus, the one whom he has sent. And as the earliest Christian communities had a vivid awareness of existing and growing under the influence of the Spirit of God, from the beginning we have the basic structure of our trinitarian faith, even if the word 'Trinity' does not appear in Greek and Latin theological vocabulary until the third century.

That is the whole concern of Christian theology in relation to God: to reconcile monotheism in the least inadequate way with the reality of the distinction of the persons in God: one God in three Persons. Even if the word Person, much reflected on in the fourth century by Basil of Caesarea and Gregory of Nazianzus, has changed meaning over centuries, as have so many human words, it would certainly be wrong to think that there are three individuals in God, more or less united in love.

Without pointing up the contrast too much, one could say that the theological tradition of the East is happier to begin from the specific nature of the Persons. The Father is not the Son; the Son is not the Father. It sees as evidence for this the spiritual attitude of Jesus towards his Father, which always respects the difference. It is at a second stage that the tradition recognizes, in faith, the mysterious unity as a victory of absolute love over all power of division.

St Augustine, Bishop of Hippo in North Africa, and therefore in the West, was more preoccupied with the risk of subordinating the Son to the Father (that was the heresy of Arius, which is still around and leaves traces in his church) than with the risk of making the Trinity uniform (the heresy of Sabellius, or modalism). He begins his reflection as a believer on the Trinity with a meditation on the mystery of the unity of God. Some Eastern theologians made the exaggerated criticism that he speaks more of the God of the philosophers than of the God of Jesus Christ. It is at a second stage that Augustine considers the distinction between the Persons and he claims that the word 'person' does not completely satisfy him.

It is the trinitarian theology of St Thomas Aquinas in the thirteenth century which represents the highest point of synthesis between the two traditions. Within his thinking St Thomas develops the idea of 'subsistent relationship'. For this great contemplative that is a way of saying in the vocabulary of his time that the mystery of the Trinity is truly that of absolute love, of the total reciprocity of love between the Father and the Son, under the influence of the Spirit. And it is in this exchange of love that we can and should live.

3　I Believe in God, the Father and Creator

The Christian dogma which proclaims that God is the creator of all things is one of the most misunderstood, and yet one of the most important in a proper presentation of the confession of faith. In particular, it is indispensable for a proper reflection on the incarnation and work of Christ the saviour. It is difficult to speak adequately of God the Creator, since at the same time one will be speaking of the creative work of humanity. We shall return to this question later.

Creation is a dogma

To say simply that God created the world because the world as we see it cannot have made itself is rationally a valuable reflection, but it is far from exhausting the believer's affirmation of the creative work of God. Besides, this creative work did not take place just at a point in time, as the starting up of a mechanism which then continues to run by itself, but is a constant divine will which keeps itself in being, allows growth and leads towards a rich fulfilment.

To affirm creation as dogma is to put it in the context of the covenant, against the broad and trustworthy horizon of the love of the Father. God does not create either out of necessity or at his whim, but in order to allow many people to participate in the living riches which are in him, 'so that many may rejoice in his light' (Preface to the fourth eucharistic prayer). Even if covenants come after creation in the history of salvation, as an offer of dialogue and communion to a partner who has to exist in order to be able to respond, it

The Alpha and the Omega. Detail of the mosaic in St Clement, Rome. Photo private collection

22

is the covenant which explains creation and not vice versa. It is the faithful love of the Father, a love which knows where it is going and which creates a future, a love which gives meaning to everything. To say that God is Creator is not to return to the past and speculate on a mysterious origin. It is to stand beside a springing fountain.

Is this dogma about the Father?

One can only answer this question by keeping in mind the maxim of the early Fathers: the works of the Trinity are common to the three Persons. You cannot divide their roles to the point of saying that one of the stages in the history of salvation concerns one Person and that the two others are not involved in it.

But it is legitimate to use the language of convenience, what academic theology calls appropriation. The work of salvation befits the Son, that of sanctification befits the Holy Spirit. In this sense it is logical to say that creation is a dogma with the Father as subject, even if it is realized in the Son by the Spirit. For the Father is the absolute source of all that exists, and it is good for us to recall that our precarious life has the same origin as the superabundant life of the eternal Son and the Spirit of love.

Bring all together in unity

We must be careful not to chop up the work of God, so that we can see as clearly as possible the unity of his plan of love. There is neither improvization nor caprice in this work of God.

This Father who is Creator is the Father of the Son, who wills from all eternity to send us his Son and recapitulate all things in him by the patient work of the Spirit. Human sin does not make him work out a new project, an emergency plan, and from the beginning the creative act is filled with the beauty of the new covenant as it is realized in Christ and by the Spirit.

To proclaim God as Creator at the beginning of our creed is thus to grasp once again, in the unity of faith, at the same time both whence we are coming and towards what future we are invited to advance.

Creation and the mystery of Easter

Nevertheless, it is in the realization of Easter,

with its dynamic death and resurrection, of burial and birth, that the new creation comes into being and is realized in the midst of the old world, with all the life-giving power of the cross. It is in the light of Easter that Paul can proclaim: 'The old world has passed away; there is a new creation' (II Cor. 5.17).

Numerous images contrast the old creation and its fulfilment in the new: the tree of the cross, which redeems the tree of the first sin, bearing green foliage and abundant fruit, like the very fine mosaic at S. Clemente in Rome. The Christ, the new Adam, in the sleep of death gives birth to the new Eve, saved humanity, born from his heart. It is a fact that Easter is a spring festival and the outpouring of victorious light within the shadows of the old world.

When we say, 'I believe in the Father, the Creator', we do well also to remember that, and to celebrate the faithful God whose love always open up a future.

Creation and Pentecost

Christ's death and resurrection are fulfilled in the mystery of Pentecost. The outpouring of the Spirit remedies the dispersion of Babel, which in the book of Genesis is the final consequence of original sin. The confusion of languages is transformed into unanimous celebrations of the wonders of God, each in his language, and the new people takes shape in this joyful confession of faith. This people does not exist for itself, but to 'celebrate the wonders of him who has called us from darkness to his marvellous light' (I Peter 2.9).

As we go on to study the creed we shall see the place of the church, as the work of the Spirit, in the service of the world, saved and loved as a whole by the Father. But we must already have our gaze on this fulfilment if we are not to make the creed a catalogue of disjointed truths. A tree in flower is not a pile of wood for burning.

New world and eucharist

This focus of the divine word on the new creation is best expressed in eucharistic celebration. It makes good sense to proclaim the Father as Creator in the course of the mass.

The assembly will take the bread, fruit of the earth and the labour of human hands, and offer it in the power of the Spirit so that it becomes the body of the living Christ. This is not a magical action, for this assembly is offering itself, so that it can become a perfect offering to the glory of the Father. Thus the fantastic project of the Father Creator goes a step forward, is accomplished in a decisive way. Thus our proclamation of faith has played its part in bringing into being the world that the Father wants for his glory and for human happiness.

4 Creators with God

We affirm that God the Father is creator of the visible universe. Human beings belong to two worlds: through our bodies we have deep roots in the visible world. And since it is in this visible universe that we live and work, we must now reflect on the way in which God acts there and in which our action can be compared to and united with his.

God alone is Creator

This affirmation must be made right away with the utmost exactness: in the strictest sense of the terms, God alone is Creator and only he can be Creator. Once we understand how much the creative act is at the root of being and comprises it, far more than being a simple starting process, this act can only be the work of God. In Hebrew the verb for create, *bara*, is used exclusively of God.

When we proclaim in the creed, 'God the Father, Creator of the visible universe', we confess in faith and praise not only that this world which surrounds us and forms the joyful and difficult, laborious and festive framework within which we live has its distant origin in God, but that it exists, now and always, in the loving purpose of this God (see the box on Providence). It is only in the framework of the confession of faith and praise that the affirmation that God is the Creator can be put in a proper way, one which does not cause anxiety. I recognize that God is the absolute and constant source of all that exists in the world and primarily of my own person, but I do so peacefully and untroubled, because in the same proclamation of faith I recognize that the source of the creative act is love.

Love produces freedom

If we thought that the intention behind the act of creation was caprice or mischance, it would not be possible to accept that this act is at the root of human freedom. A jealous or perverse God could not encourage the freedom of his creatures.

But if love is the root of all creation, there is no longer anything to fear, from either God nor man. This is a human freedom which grows and flourishes within the freedom for self-expression that God confers on it. It is a freedom which is contextual but real. Far from being limited externally by the omnipotence of God, it finds in God himself the foundation of its growth.

Although we should remember that only God is Creator, we should also find in this affirmation the sure foundation of the creativity of human beings who create with God, a creativity which includes the spiritual adventure and the realization of our salvation.

Creators with God

The artist who produces a new work, for example a poem or a piece of music, is not a creator in the sense that God is. He gives new structures to sound or literary material, beautiful and harmonious forms, but he does not give them absolute existence. And above all, he does not retain that permanent bond with his work which would prevent him from creating a new one. However, he or she is a creator with God, to the degree that he or she cooperates in this harmonization of the world which makes it a pleasant place for human beings, a reflection of the divine beauty. And when what comes to be expressed says much more about anguish, then it is an expression of the precarious character of our world.

When parents give birth to a new being, reflection must be even more sophisticated and profound. This is no longer creation in the strict sense, since the new being which the parents

The creation of birds and fish. Detail. Cathedral of Monreale, 1174–1182. Photo private collection

produce differs from both of them and will have his or her own spiritual adventure, again different from theirs. The specific task of education is to provide an apprenticeship in freedom which does not tie the child too closely to those who have given it life.

One cannot say that at the moment of conception parents transmit bodily life and that God reserves to himself the creation of the soul, as if one could divide up the roles in this way, forgetting that God is also fully the creator of the body.

So all we can do is to return to this certainty that divine love is the creator of freedom. God gives life, and it is by love that he gives living beings the capacity to produce life. It is in cooperation with his creative action that parents bring new life to birth, and if they are Christians, they know that their child receives both all their love and all God's love.

Male and female he made them

'God created man in his image, in the image of God he created him' (Gen. 1.26). We all know this text, but we have difficulty in attaching importance to it. If human beings are in the image of God – and that is our greatest claim to glory, the reassuring foundation of our spiritual adventure – we do not realize this vocation in solitude. From the beginning God wants this adventure to be realized in the personal community, in the image of his own trinitarian communion, and primarily in the Church, that privileged community of men and women.

We should not idealize things, even in connection with paradise: the communities of persons are demanding, and go against the fear of losing oneself and the instinct of self-preservation that we all have. They call for a courageous acceptance of the other in his or her irreducible difference. Personal community is not an idyllic tête-a-tête, but inevitably leads to conflict.

That having been said and quietly accepted, loving communion of individuals expresses the will of God for humanity. 'The definitive creation of humanity consists in the creation of the unity of two beings . . . The complete and definitive creation of humanity (primarily subject to the experience of original solitude) is expressed in the fact of giving life to this personal communion in which men and women are involved' (John-Paul II, audience of 14 November 1979).

The Christian significance of the body

This personal communion can only be realized through the medium of the body, for the body reveals the person. John-Paul II recalled that in this same audience and all through his teaching on sexuality with phrases the precision and realism of which might easily shock prudes. For the Church cannot despise the body without the risk of doing harm to the creative power of its God. And it must not forget that it is the Church of the incarnate Word, the Son of God who became flesh.

The task of the Church to teach and claim this Christian significance of the body is a delicate one at a time when the Church is immersed in a world which, at least in the West, often confuses body and pleasure, sexuality and eroticism. But for all that the church does not have the right to renounce biblical realism: 'And the man and his wife were both naked, and were not ashamed' (Gen. 2.25). And we should rejoice to see that the one who at present presides over its missionary course does not cultivate false modesty in the slightest.

The couple express their communion by means of the body. 'The body manifests the reciprocity and the communion of persons. It expresses this in giving, as a fundamental characteristic of personal existence. That is what the body is: a witness to creation as a fundamental gift. So it is a witness to love as a source, from which is born the very fact of giving' (Audience of 9 January 1980).

God gives the woman to the man. Detail of the door of Hildesheim cathedral.
Photo Bild Archiv – Foto Marburg (Ziolo)

An image of the communion of the Trinity

For it is at this level that revelation is achieved. And despite all its opaqueness, the body becomes the place of revelation of God the Spirit.

In its capacity for expression it becomes the gift of the person.

We always have to return to the mystery of the Trinity. If the human couple has a capacity and a mission to reveal God, it is because God himself is not characterized by imprisonment in solitude,

---

God is creating today

As we have said, creation is not just a matter of an initial flick of the fingers. It comes about through what we call providence. The word 'create' is not conjugated in the past.

Entrusted to the loving care of God

Fr Rahner suggested this happy and fine phrase to describe providence: 'We are entrusted to the loving care of God.' Divine providence is more than a maintenance agreement by which a firm undertakes to ensure that a piece of office equipment functions properly.

God's providence is the safeguard of a faithful love. God is truly preoccupied with each one of his creatures; he keeps them all alive to the degree necessary for their spiritual growth or flourishing. Even if we do not know exactly how this preoccupation affects God and is in harmony with his infinite happiness, we must remember that this preoccupation is a real one because the love of the Father is strong and constant. God never just pretends to love us.

To affirm the providence of the Father is to give full scope to our confession of faith: God creates through love. In this way we avoid the trap which would consist in thinking that the act of creation is only a matter of getting everything started, after which God leaves his work to itself without bothering about it. God is never disin-

terested in any of his works. Even the sinner – and we are all sinners – may be confident of the loving care of God. And it is because of this providence that we ourselves, if we want to be the children of this Father who makes his sun rise on the just and the unjust (Matt. 5.45), cannot be uninterested in any of our brothers and sisters. We must even respect the world and nature that are entrusted to us. A proper Christian understanding of ecology begins here.

A liberating Providence

It would be wrong to see the Father's Providence as being finickity and stifling. We know very well that a mother does not bring up her children well, is bad for them, if she prevents them from maturing and developing.

God's providence is liberating because God wants the growth of beings until they achieve spiritual maturity. God does not create for the sake of creating but to give life. He is truly an educator of men and women in the greatest sense of this word, which means 'lead beyond'.

It is in this perspective of faith that believers learn to assume their responsibilities, that they take over their lives and make free choices, without always looking for the support of someone else's written law to tell them what they are to do, in the name of God.

but by mysterious communion. It is not that trinitarian communion is modelled on the experience of marriage, and catechists are well aware of the trap of speaking of the Trinity as a family. But we must not be afraid of saying how much married love, when experienced as self-giving and concern for the other, contributes to showing us the God of Jesus, where 'the Son does nothing that he does not see the Father doing', and where the Father himself does not preserve his intimacy jealously, but gives all to the Son whom he loves. This total and reciprocal gift is lived out in the love of the Spirit. And this Spirit also dwells in us: he dwells in every human being who honestly lives out the adventure of true love.

5 I Believe in God, Creator of Humanity

Even if part of humanity is bound up with the visible world, and if we have already reflected on human beings as sharing with God in creation, we must now reflect more carefully on the relationship between human beings and their God.

A paradoxical being

The humane sciences have shown us more and more of the bundle of paradoxes and tensions of which human beings are made up. These paradoxes and tensions keep us from making over-simple statements: human beings are never 'nothing but this or nothing but that'. Each of us is well aware that he or she is capable of both better and worse, and there is no authentic spiritual progress without this courageous awareness.

By this route the humane sciences rejoin the course of the Bible, which is neither naive nor despairing on the subject of human beings. Certainly human beings rejoice at being a 'wonderful creation' (Ps. 137), but the biblical history tells us enough of the cowardice of which human beings are capable.

What revelation teaches us, and what science cannot tell us, is the profound theological cause of these conflicts and this paradox. For human beings come from God, and as St Augustine and St Bernard were well aware, they cannot completely lose the memory of their origin, even if they lose their way in the 'land of dissimilarity'. The Bible expresses this with the theme of the image: 'God made man in his image, after his likeness' (Gen. 1.26). The Eastern tradition, after Irenaeus of Lyons, has been careful about the

Adam. Detail of the polyptych by Van Eyck. Ghent cathedral. Photo private collection

Eve. Detail. Lucas Cranach the Elder, 1472–1553. Antwerp. Photo private collection

31

distinction between these two words:

The divine *image* in man is absolute and cannot be lost, even through sin. So the Eastern tradition has always been preserved from the exaggerated pessimism of Martin Luther and has never recognized the total corruption of nature.

It is the *likeness* which is affected by sin. It is as a result of sin that human beings risk being lost in the land of dissimilarity of which Pope Gregory the Great spoke at the beginning of the seventh century. The Christian life is a progressive restoration of the likeness. The likeness gradually becomes more real by the acceptance of grace, the welcoming of the Word and the life of the sacraments.

Human beings must live out this constant adventure of being conformed to Christ within this world which is their world, with the burden of their heredity, their environment and their bodily condition. All this is not necessarily an obstacle and can even become a support, but it creates a burden which brings with it the risk of being closed in on oneself and becoming egotistic. That is why the spiritual adventure is a struggle; not that God wants to see us suffer in order to test our strength, but because we are not at the end of the road.

Are we soul and body?

This spiritual combat should not be presented as that of the body against the soul, since that would lead us to scorn the body, which is also the work of the creator God.

Besides, the division between soul and body is too narrow and too rigid to come near to the paradoxical truth of being a human being. We need not reject it completely on the grounds that it originated in Greek philosophy and not in biblical thought. But we must not forget that the Christians of the East have a more subtle anthropology with three terms: spirit, soul and body. Above all we must not forget that human beings are not composites, a soul using a body as a simple instrument of which it can dispose: human beings do not *have* bodies, but *are* bodies, as a means of expressing their spiritual richness. And we do not have to speculate on what human features there could be in a body without a soul or a soul without a body (See chapter 29 on the resurrection of the flesh, page 146).

Nature and vocation

Perhaps we do not need to dwell on excessively static definitions of humanity. Rather, we should consider human vocation, the task which we have to fulfil in the world, in fellowship with our brothers and sisters and in the presence of our God. Our age, so concerned for efficiency, may be sensitive to such an approach.

Every human being comes into the world with a task to accomplish. The Father establishes us as it were in a garden which is to be cultivated and kept (Gen. 2.15), so that we realize a community of love, worthy both of God and humanity, and thus go our own way towards meeting the love of the Father.

It is less important to know precisely what we are – for human beings will be a mystery to the end – than to know what is offered to us and asked of us. On condition that we never forget that our God has not hurled us into the adventure of life to cope with it alone, but gives us the power of the Spirit day by day.

6 God, Creator of the Invisible World

I believe in one God, the Father almighty, Creator of the universe, visible and invisible. It would not be correct on our part to skirt round this affirmation without seeking to understand what it means in the confession of faith.

For men and women of the ancient world, whether pagan or Christian, the visible world was surrounded by the invisible world. The Bible and the Gospels, like all the spiritual books of antiquity, no matter what their origin, are full of allusions to the angles and the powers. But they affirm with great force:

God is the creator of everything: no created power can ultimately oppose his power.

The Risen Christ is Lord, 'raised above the angels'.

What the angels cannot be

We shall find it easier to speak of angels if we first firmly rule out certain wrong ideas.

The angels, or messengers of God, are not kinds of mysterious powers, relatively independent of God, with which we have to come to terms independently of our relationship with God himself. We shall be spelling that out in more detail when we come to discuss the devil. Whatever angels may be, they are creatures like us, objects of God's good providence. Nor should they be invoked to avoid the test of encountering God himself.

We know that God is infinitely near, that he has a loving concern for each one of us and that we cannot consider the angels as being a counterbalance to the absoluteness of God. It has not always been like this, and in the ancient religions the angels could be considered to be intermediary powers, forming a screen between the puny poverty of human beings and the majesty of an inaccessible God. The incarnation of the beloved Son prohibits us from dividing out roles in this way. And if in Christian theology the angels have a function, a task, a ministry, it cannot be that of dispensing us from encounter with the God of love, manifested in Christ.

The angels are at the service of humanity

For when we speak of angels we are speaking of service and ministry. 'Are they not all ministering spirits sent forth to serve?' (Heb. 1.14).

They are messengers of God towards us, making known his love and helping us to understand his plan of salvation better. They are also our teachers, showing us how to keep our gaze fixed on the Lord. The prophet Ezekiel has this fine saying about the angels: 'They went, without turning as they went' (Ezek. 1.12). This is the stability of a created existence, wholly orientated on the contemplation of the love of the Lord. And for us, who come and go, who try to keep our gaze on the Lord but often turn our back on him, turning ourselves away, this is a valuable reminder of the one thing that is necessary.

The ministry of the angels among us is close to that of the saints whom we love to invoke: they too have their gaze fixed on the Lord, and see everything in the light of his love. Devotion to a guardian angel should be connected with the invocation of the one whose name we have borne since our baptism.

The angels are subject to Christ

This is perhaps the most important thing to recall in a Christian confession of faith, as we are about to set out to read what our creed proclaims about Christ.

'He who was for a little while made lower than the angels, crowned with glory and honour because of the suffering of death, so that by the grace of God he might taste death for every one' (Heb. 2.9). For the Fathers of the church (and for any theology aware of what it affirms and what it must leave in the shade), the revolt of an angel cannot directly put in question the majesty of God. But it can be jealousy against humanity, a rejection of this 'insane love' of God for humanity, this love which could make possible the incarnation, to the point of the humiliation of the cross.

The risen Jesus takes his place as the Lord of the visible and invisible world. 'As head, the Christ is not only the vital principle of the church, but is also the one who dominates all the cosmic powers' (Lohfink). Paul had a vivid awareness of this recapitulation in Christ, a recapitulation which goes well beyond humanity and what we can see. Perhaps we have to rediscover the balance of this vision of faith: everything is subject to Christ, but this Lordship of Christ over all the universe goes far beyond what we can imagine.

An angel. Detail of the mosaic in the choir of the Carolingian church of Germigny-des-Près (806). Photo private collection

34

7   God is not the Creator of Evil

Our creeds do not say anything about evil, that problem which has preoccupied men and women from the beginning. Is that contempt for our anxieties? If God is good, could one dare to say that evil does not really exist, that it is only a semblance? Is this not rather an invitation to go further, beyond the illusion of words?

The illusion of words

For if vocabulary ever runs the risk of giving us illusions, it does so above all when we come to evil. We combine such different realities under the same word! We call evil a marriage which breaks up because of selfishness or an earthquake which claims the lives of millions of innocent victims. Is this the same evil? This young man in agony, victim of an incurable disease, is a victim of evil, but so is the person in the next bed who was stabbed in a fight, the loneliness of an old person who is dying and the racial injustice which never comes to an end. We are well aware that we are talking of very different realities, because human responsibility is not always involved to the same degree, and because we cannot conceive of the intervention of the good God always in the same way.

God wants only good

St Thomas Aquinas proclaims in his balanced and wise theological synthesis that the God of Christians does not have the idea of evil. He, who is all goodness, wants only good, and could not positively will evil as the inevitable shadow-side of his love. He cannot even calculate evil to put human love to the test. Our God is no Machiavelli, and to say that he allows evil is already to have gone a long way.

What is perhaps more correct is to recognize that the God of love can take the risk of love. His creative work is already an immense risk, since it produces a world which has its own laws, its internal evolution in which sometimes a person may be crushed. That does not mean that this person ceases to be loved. He is loved by God, this invalid who suffers apparently for no good reasons, even if it is difficult to discern that love. And God accepts the supreme risk when he faces human freedom, capable of saying no to his love and choosing revolt.

And even in the face of this refusal, God will continue to love humanity and to give us a sign. This sign will often be a very subtle sign, and we must accept the silence of Job. The Bible is full of formulas which express this constant care of the God of the covenant for sinful humanity. In the face of our sin God remains our advocate, our defender. He is the best defender of humanity faced with the destructive madness which can sometimes seize hold of us. The first chapters of Genesis, in particular chapter 3, are an eloquent indication of how, when humanity chooses to say no to God, it takes the road of its own unhappiness. And how even when we depart from him, God continues to love us and invites us to return to him.

In Jesus there is only 'Yes'

I am very fond of this saying of Paul about Christ (II Cor. 1.19). Jesus only tells us the Father's 'Yes' to our flourishing and our happiness. He does not offer us two equal routes, as the shopkeeper offers us a choice between two household appliances, each with its advantages and its disadvantages.

Jesus shows the truth and the coherence of the Father's plan: he proclaims that the Father knows humankind and that he knows by what way we can truly find fulfilment. This way is that of cross and resurrection, of the gift of our selves, and even if it seems rough, it is a fine and good road: 'It is better to give than to receive' (Acts 20.35), said Jesus in a saying which Paul has handed down to us and which illuminates the course of all human beings, not just that of Christians. Millions of men and women try this course who have never heard the teaching of Christ, and who experience its truth in their everyday choices.

It is the true way of human happiness for the tremendous yet simple reason that it is what God experiences constantly in his love, which is always generous and always unmerited.

The devil is a creature

That is the first affirmation to be made if we are to have a balanced faith. It is reassuring and liberating. In the confession of Christian faith the devil cannot be presented as an occult power, as strong as God, dividing the world into equal parts with him. He is no longer the prince of this world; he has already been overthrown (John 12.31). And his final defeat is the certainty of our faith in the risen Christ.

'Anyone who makes the devil a separate principle, not even having his origin with God, like any other creature, departs from the framework of the teaching of the Bible and the Church' (Paul VI, Audience of 15 November 1972).

And Cardinal Ratzinger, who recalls this teaching, makes it even more specific: 'By themselves, human beings themselves do not have the strength to oppose Satan; but Satan is not another God. In union with Jesus, we have the certainty that we shall conquer him.' Those who see the work of the devil everywhere, who speak only of dies that are cast, and who too easily resort to exorcists, must remember the reassuring balance of this teaching.

Yes, the devil exists and acts

This should put us at ease over recognizing and confessing that the devil really exists: 'For Christian faith the devil is a presence which is mysterious but real, personal and not just symbolic.'

It is above all within the abyss of our hearts that we must recognize and discern this active presence: 'The devil is the enemy number one, he is the tempter *par excellence*. So we know that this obscure and disturbing being truly exists and still acts. He is the specious tempter of the moral equilibrium of humanity. He is the treacherous enchanter who knows how to insinuate himself into us to lead us astray' (Paul VI, 15 November 1972). The Pastor of the Church does not remind us of that to make us worried, but to awaken our faith in the victorious Christ.

The first temptation of Christ. Capital of the twelfth-century cathedral of Autun. Photo private collection

8   Creation Waits for Christ

Christianity is a religion of the future. It is important to say that once again at the end of this first part which has directed us above all towards the mystery of our first beginnings. We have been reflecting on what lies behind us only in order to summon our energies for the journey onwards, just as the runner puts all his or her weight on the starting block so as to press off towards the finishing tape.

The expectation of the kingdom

This is what we must talk about first, this expectation of the presence in which everything will finally be realized because God will be all in all (I Cor. 15.28). We are not the only ones to be waiting. In a very mysterious chapter Paul evokes this expectation of creation which groans and sighs, waiting for deliverance (Rom. 8.22). No proper proclamation of Christian faith can fail to include his ardent desire, 'Maranatha, Come, Lord Jesus' (I Cor. 16.22; Rev. 22.20). The *aggiornamento* is in process of restoring to Catholicism this prayer which is so full of hope, and that is a good thing, for we must not allow the sects to monopolise it: we must proclaim it without anxiety, and allow it to rise up from the depths of our hearts.

For nothing is yet accomplished, and we proclaim our faith in the most intimate of our hopes. The creed itself has a place within a eucharistic celebration which always has something of a nocturnal vigil about it, watching intently for the joyful cry of full deliverance: 'Behold the bridegroom comes. Go out to meet him' (Matt. 25.26). The proclamation of faith sustains waiting, revives vigilance, and even if it sends us back to the performance of everyday tasks, its aim is not to quench desire.

He who must come

The Old Testament is underpinned by the expectation of the one who will inaugurate the New Covenant, which will not be engraved on tables of stone but inscribed in the depths of our hearts (Jer. 31). We cannot say how much our faith in God the Father and Creator follows the riches and the quest of that of Israel without ending this first part with a reference to Jesus.

Granted, we have put him in parentheses in these pages. But to end with, we must say how much our faith is Christian, even and above all when it speaks of the Father. Otherwise we would give the false impression of having opened this book with a philosophical reflection. All that we have just said has been affirmed in the light of the teaching of Jesus, and we have time to say something more explicitly about him, the one who must come.

We must not forget that we are proclaiming the whole creed in the faith of the Church which is the work of the Holy Spirit. It is he who supports the whole of our confession of faith and who sends us out into the world to proclaim the wonders of the one who has brought us out of darkness into his marvellous light (I Peter 2.9).

PART TWO

9   And in One Lord Jesus Christ

'You believe in God, believe also in me', says Jesus (John 14.1). At the centre of our creed, the second part, the longest, expresses our faith in Jesus Christ. Is this as it were a second faith to be added to our faith in God which is expressed in the first part of the creed? What is the significance of the 'and' which links these two parts of the text?

Is faith in God split into three?

'And in one Lord Jesus Christ,' proclaims the Greek text of the Nicene Creed. The Latin translation has kept this conjunction: *Et in unum Dominum . . . Et in Jesus Christum* is the simple expression of the Apostles' Creed. This *et* is a good expression of Jesus' 'also' in St John. In our

---

Two ways of reading the creed

The text of the Niceno-Constantinopolitan creed can be read in two ways, both in conformity with the faith of the Church but presenting two different approaches to the mystery of the Trinity.

The Latin tradition more usually begins from an affirmation of the oneness of God, what it calls the one divine nature, and then goes on to develop the trinity of persons. We could present this way of reading the creed as follows:

I believe in one God { the Father / the Son / the Holy Spirit

A good example of this Latin approach is the creed of Paul VI, which has a complete first part about God before even speaking of the Father, the Son and the Spirit. We find the same thing in some forms of blessing: 'May Almighty God bless you, the Father, the Son and the Holy Spirit.'

The Greek tradition begins more spontaneously with an affirmation of the three Persons. For it, one God, the Father, is the source of divinity. Moreover, that is the way in which the New Testament writers expressed their belief. That produces the following pattern:

I believe in one God, the Father,
and in one Lord Jesus Christ
and in the Holy Spirit.

Of course the Latin tradition has to avoid making the one God, put first, into a kind of fourth person. And the Greek tradition has to stress emphatically that the Son and the Spirit are one with the Father, of the same nature, to avoid at the same time affirming three gods, and conceiving of the Son and Spirit as being inferior to the Father. In the Greek world, that was the main issue for the councils of Nicaea and Constantinople.

modern liturgical translation we have brought this out by a repetition of 'I believe', which is repeated again for the Holy Spirit.

In the great liturgy of Easter night, when it is asked about its faith in Father, Son and Spirit, the community replies three times 'We believe', just as the catechumen presented for baptism proclaims 'I believe' three times. Not as a faith broken into three pieces, a faith twice bisected, but as the trinal, trinitarian expression of a unique faith, a redoubled faith in the one God. One Lord, one faith, one baptism (Eph. 4.5). We do not have three faiths; we believe in one thrice-holy God.

Beginning from Jesus

This second part of the creed speaks of Jesus. It gives him his human name. It is only as Jesus that the only-begotten Son of God has been made known to us. The fathers of the Church did not seek to speculate on a second Person of the Trinity about whose life a hypothesis might have been made independently of the life, death and resurrection of Jesus. It is important to be clear about that. For if the Apostles' Creed begins very clearly from Jesus ('And in Jesus Christ, his only begotten Son our Lord, who was conceived'), the Nicene Creed might give the impression of first speaking of the eternal Son and only going on to the incarnation at a second stage when it continues: 'For us men and for our salvation . . . he was made man.' We shall try to understand how the demands of controversy and the defence of the faith led to a stress on the true nature of Jesus Christ from the very first lines. But the one it is about is Jesus, the one whom the first disciples had followed and known on the roads of Palestine. To speak of the Trinity outside the human and earthly destiny of Jesus is always to risk becoming fanciful.

So the creed only speaks of Jesus of Nazareth, even when what it says goes beyond the horizon of the earthly destiny of Jesus. But it immediately says of this Jesus that he is Christ; it speaks of him in a Christian way. To speak of Jesus is not in fact the monopoly of Christians. Millions of people, here and now, have never heard of the Jesus whom we call the Lord of all. They have never been able to speak of him. But within the cultural ambit of Christianity over twenty centuries many people have sought to say something about Jesus without offering allegiance to him. They have even been able to speak of him with rigour and competence, as historians or philosophers. Our originality, which the creed has to show, is that we speak of Jesus whom we recognize as Christ: we speak of him as Christians, as his followers.

Jesus

In Hebrew, Yehoshua, Joshua, which in Greek becomes Jesus, means 'God saves', or 'God is salvation'. This name, revealed to Mary (Luke 1.31), expresses the mission and identity of her son. In him and not only by him, God saves.

Jesus is God who saves the world. By conferring this name on him Joseph exercises an authentic legal paternity in respect of Jesus (Matt. 1.21) and thus brings him into the genealogy of David. God's salvation is incorporated into our history.

Christ-Messiah

In Hebrew, *mashiach* denotes the one who is marked out for a particular mission, consecrated by being anointed with oil. This is what happened to kings, like David, but also to the high priests. In the Greek translation of the Bible *mashiach* became *christos* (from *chriein*, anoint). Hence the two English words which are more transcriptions than translations: messiah, from *mashiach*, and Christ, from *Christos*.

In later Judaism the messiah is the one who is expected for the restoration of the people of Israel and to inaugurate the kingdom of God, according to the promises made to the descendants of David (Gen. 49.10; Num. 24.17; II Sam. 7; Pss. 2; 72; 110).

The disciples of Jesus recognize him as the Messiah, the sole Christ (Acts 2.33–36), to the point of making that his proper name, and even call themselves *Christianoi* (Acts 11.26). But Jesus himself seems to mistrust this title because of the excessively narrow political and national interpretation that his contemporaries gave to it. Jesus accepts it at his passion (Mark 14.62), at a time when there was no risk of misunderstanding the nature of the power which he claimed.

The only one

What difference does that make? To say that Jesus is Christ, Messiah, could identify him as one emissary of God among others. But Jesus is not only Christ, Messiah: he is the Messiah, the Christ. We shall constantly find this definite article prefacing the titles given to Jesus: the Lamb of God, the Servant, the Son of Man, the Son of God. By itself, then, this article is more evocative than the title, the significance of which is always open to discussion, or which can be elaborated in such a way as to fit others. But for Christians Jesus is not an emissary of God, a prophet, a servant, someone with a mandate, a messiah, among many others in a series. For us he is the one and only person to be that, or to be it at this point.

So, by setting Jesus apart in this way when they speak of him, Christians also set themselves apart. When they speak of Jesus they also say something about themselves. Saying that Jesus alone is Christ, they profess their identity as Christians. So the originality of Christians does not lie in what they try to do for others. (What more do we have, they often ask themselves, when so many non-Christians do the same thing, or do it much better?) Their originality is no longer a matter of believing in God or even believing in one God: they share this faith at least with Jews and Moslems. Their only originality, their identity, is to believe that the oneness of God is represented (and not betrayed) by the sole Lordship of Jesus Christ.

Christ is Lord

For the Lordship of Christ is that of God. In New Testament Greek Kyrios, Lord, is not a simple courtesy title, as if the disciples or the individuals met by Jesus called him 'Sir'. It is truly a name which is proper to God, the Lord God, Adonai, of the Old Testament. It really took all the boldness of Paul to dare to transfer to Jesus the affirmation of the prophet Joel, 'Whoever shall call on the name of the Lord will be saved' (Joel 3.5, quoted in Rom. 10.9). From now on, for the apostles, that becomes true of the one who calls Jesus Lord. That is the song of praise in the

Christ Pantocrator. Byzantine mosaic. Palatine chapel, Palermo.
Photo Roger-Viollet-Anderson

Christian liturgy: 'That every tongue may proclaim that Jesus Christ is Lord to the glory of God the Father' (Phil. 2.11). But in us such a profession of faith can only be the fruit of the Spirit:, 'No one can say that Jesus Christ is Lord but by the Holy Spirit' (I Cor. 12.3).

For us the word lord has feudal connotations: a lord and his vassals. In a hierarchical society, where the lord himself has more powerful lords above him, he dominates those whom he protects. It was quite natural in the Middle Ages for the Lordship of Jesus Christ sometimes to have been understood on this model: he is our supreme sovereign and Mary is Our Lady. Besides, this affirmation retains something of its significance when we remember that Christians suffered death to proclaim that Christ and not Caesar was Lord.

Lord

God told his name, YHWH, to Moses and his people (Ex. 3.14). In Judaism the name is more than a designation. It presents, hands over, the person himself or herself. Human beings are not to abuse this vulnerability of God (Ex. 20.7). In Israel the name of God became the object of such veneration that people stopped daring to pronounce it in the public reading of scripture. Where YHWH was written, people said Adonai, Lord. And in the Greek translation of the Bible Kyrios, Lord, became the proper name of God.

So to call Jesus Kyrios, Lord, is to put him on the same level as God, to accord him the name which is above every name, the name that God himself confers on his Son (Phil. 2.9). The formula 'Jesus Christ is Lord' is one of the confessions of faith most used by the first Christian communities (Acts 2.36; Rom. 10.9; I Cor. 12.3; II Cor. 1.2; 4.5; Phil. 2.11). It expresses the divinity of Jesus.

As a servant

But if the Lordship of Jesus is a sovereignty and a reign, it is so in a very special way: 'You call me Teacher and Lord, and you are right, for that is what I am' (John 13.13), says Jesus the very moment when the act of service which he has just performed has swept away all possible alternative meanings to the title of Lord. The action of Jesus in going down on his knees before his disciples to wash their feet does not deny or contradict his Lordship, and does not even put it in parentheses for a moment. On the contrary, it is unveiled, revealed for what it is: not domination or omnipotence, but service. Or rather, it is the domination and omnipotence of self-giving love. And if Jesus has no other Lordship than that of his God and Father, there finally, as throughout the passion of Jesus, God, though apparently thwarted, is still fully Lord.

Enthroned in his resurrection

In his Lordship Jesus does not supplant the Father: he refers everything to him. If he is Lord, he is Lord to the glory of God the Father and not in his stead. 'When all things are subject to him,' St Paul comments, 'then the Son himself will also be subjected to him who put all things under him, that God may be everything to everyone' (I Cor. 15.28).

And it is in the resurrection of Jesus that his Lordship is fully inaugurated, as a victory over evil, a triumph over death, the negation of the power of hatred. 'This Jesus whom you crucified, God has made Lord and Christ,' proclaims Peter on the day of Pentecost, contrasting the work of God with that of the inhabitants of Jerusalem and their rulers (Acts 2.36).

Monotheism is a combat

To proclaim that Jesus is Lord is not just a liturgical acclamation; it is first of all a refusal of, and therefore a combat against, all in this world that might proclaim itself Lord, beginning with the prince of this world. It is a declaration of war on all forms of idolatry, in a direct line with the affirmation which opens our creed: God alone is God. The victory of Jesus Christ over evil and death bears witness that God alone is God, the God whose Lordship Jesus inaugurates, the God whose kingdom he ushers in. Like all the affirmations of monotheism, then, the confession of faith 'Christ is Lord' implies a particular kind of behaviour, of life-style. For if we believe

45

in one Lord Jesus Christ, that means that for us Caesar is not lord, that money is not lord, nor progress, nor sex, nor the class struggle. To say that Jesus is Lord is to affirm in a way which is both compromising and liberating that from now on nothing will any longer dominate our lives.

The Father's last word

And this lordship is definitive. It inaugurates the reign of God promised for the end of time. So there is nothing and no one else to look for. 'Are you he who should come or do we look for another?' The question of those sent by John the Baptist (Matt. 11.3) is that of many of our contemporaries, always in quest of some new revelation. But as St John of the Cross put it very well, in a period which in this respect resembled our own, Jesus is the last word of God, in whom from now on everything has been said (see the box). We are still threatened, and perhaps we shall be even more so towards the end of the twentieth century, by millennarian currents which imagine, sometimes by interpreting scripture wrongly, a new age which will no longer be that of Jesus, the unique Messiah of God. But in anything to do with the work of the Spirit, or in any confidence imparted by the Virgin Mary, whatever is in accordance with God can only fit in with the unique Lordship of Jesus Christ.

God's last word

The principal reason why in the law of Scripture the enquiries that were made of God were lawful, and why it was fitting that prophets and priests should seek visions and revelations of God, was because at that time faith had no firm foundation, neither was the law of the gospel established; and thus it was needful that men should enquire of God and that he should speak, whether by words or by visions and revelations or whether by figures and similitudes or by many other ways of expressing his meaning. For all that he answered and spake and revealed belonged to the mysteries of our faith and things touching it or leading to it . . .

But now that the faith is founded on Christ and, in this era of grace, the law of the Gospel has been made manifest, there is no need to enquire of him in that manner nor for him to speak or answer as he did then. For in giving us, as he did, his Son, which is his Word – and he has no other – he spoke to us all together, once and for all, in this single Word, and he has no occasion to speak further.

And this is the sense of that passage with which Saint Paul begins, when he tries to persuade the Hebrews that they should abandon those first manners and ways of converse with God which are in the law of Moses and should set their eyes on Christ alone, saying, 'In many and various ways God spoke of old to our fathers by the prophets; but in these last days he has spoken to us by a Son.' Herein the apostle declares that God has become as it were dumb, and has no more to say, since that which he spoke aforetime, in part, to the prophets, he has now spoken altogether in him, giving us the all, which is his Son. Wherefore he that would now enquire of God, or seek any vision or revelation, would not only be acting foolishly but would be committing an offence against God, by not setting his eyes altogether upon Christ, and seeking no new thing nor aught beside.

St John of the Cross, *Ascent of Mount Carmel*, 2.22.3–5 in *The Complete Works of St John of the Cross*, Vol. 1, 162f., Burns and Oates 1935

10　The Only Son of God

'Truly this man was the Son of God' (Mark 15.39). In the Gospel of Mark, it is the Roman officer in charge of the execution of Jesus who, seeing the way in which he died, proclaims in this way what will be the faith of all Christians in Jesus the Son of God. No one will ever know what the centurion meant by these words. But as the evangelist understood the words, it was the pagans who, by the cross, in this way arrived at the heart of the faith.

In his resurrection

Jesus seems to have avoided using this title, doubtless because of its ambiguity on the Jewish tradition. After his resurrection, when the community recognized him as Christ and Lord, it also recognized him as the true Son of God.

Son of God is primarily a title for after Easter. It is after his resurrection that Jesus is enthroned in this dignity as Son of God, and right at the

---

Who is Son of God?

In the Old Testament this name is given to the angels (Job 1.6; 2.1; 38.7) or to mysterious superior powers (Gen. 6.2). For human beings the title seems to have been primarily kept for the king at his enthronement (Isa. 9.5; Ps. 2.7; 89.27; 110.3). It is with this logic that it was then given to the heir of David, the Messiah (II Sam. 7.14).

But the people of Israel is also called son of God (in the singular: Ex. 4.22; Hos. 11.1; Jer. 31.20; or in the plural: Hos. 2.1; Isa. 1.2; Jer. 3.19). So this title perhaps indicates less sonship in the strict sense than the attachment, the tenderness, the care, the education given by God as a father. It is in this lesser sense that Jesus himself spoke of those who make peace, or of those who love their enemies, as sons of God, sons of the Most High (Matt. 5.9; Luke 6.35).

The name Son of God takes on an original meaning in the New Testament: it expresses an absolutely unique relationship with God which characterizes Jesus from the beginning (Luke 1.35). John spoke of the Only Son, Monogenes (John 1.14; 1.18; 3.16; 3.18; I John 4.9).

This title of Jesus, revealed by God himself (Mark 1.11; 9.7), divulged by the demons (Mark 3.11; 5,7), according to John at the heart of the controversy (5.18–20; 10.33; 19.7), is only accepted by Jesus himself at the time of his trial (Luke 22.70).

Following Jesus, those who live by his Spirit are also sons of God (Rom. 8.14). However, to distinguish this sonship by participation in the unique Sonship of Jesus John prefers to use another word and call them children of God (John 1.12; 11.52; I John 3.1–2, 10; 5.2).

beginning of the Letter to the Romans, St Paul can sum up the good news that he wanted to pass on to them as 'the gospel of God, which he promised beforehand through his prophets in the holy scriptures, the gospel concerning his Son, who was descended from David according to the flesh and designated Son of God in power according to his resurrection from the dead, Jesus Christ our Lord' (Rom. 1.2–4). Paul does not mean to say that at his resurrection Jesus became Son of God whereas he was not before (the gospel of God is about God's Son), but he distinguishes two times, two stages, in the career of Jesus: his earthly life according to the flesh and his Easter glorification in his resurrection. It is then that the son of David is enthroned as Son of God and receives all his prerogatives.

God had promised him

That was the expectation of the Jewish people. They knew that their kings were the treasured sons of the Most High, and several psalms celebrating the son of God doubtless had their origin in the royal enthronement ceremony. God himself in some way adopted the royal heir and made him sit at his right hand. Then they sang: 'Oracle of the Lord (God) to my Lord (the king): Sit at my right hand, until I make your enemies your footstool' (Ps. 110.1; cf. also Ps. 2). They looked forward to the day when this promise was realized in full for the descendant of David, so that God truly became a Father who would finally accept full life in the Son: 'I will be to him a father and he shall be to me a son,' the Lord had promised by the prophet Nathan (II Sam. 7.14).

In the resurrection of Jesus, with the light of the Spirit, the disciples of Jesus understood that the ancient promise had already been realized beyond their imagining. The son of David is truly the Son of God: 'What God promised to the fathers, this he has fulfilled to us their children by raising Jesus; as also it is written in the second psalm: Thou art my Son, today I have begotten

thee' (Acts 13.33; quoting Ps. 2.7). This begetting, this birth, is the resurrection of Jesus, as his entry into the very life of God, with the assurance that from Jesus onwards it is to be communicated further. 'To those who received him, to those who believe in his name, he gave the power to become children of God' (John 1.12). Hence one can understand why, after his baptism at Damascus, Paul hastened to go round the synagogues to proclaim that Jesus is the Son of God (Acts 9.20).

The supreme ease of the Son

But, for the first generation of disciples, as for Christians who recite the creed today, to proclaim Jesus as the only Son of God is not just to affirm his resurrection. This title Son illuminates his life and his death, and tells us something of his very being, of his nature.

One might even suppose that for the apostles, illuminated by the Easter glorification of Jesus and by the gift of the Holy Spirit at Pentecost, this title Son of God was *a posteriori* a kind of key which allowed them to see the coherence, the filial logic, of the whole life of Jesus. They had been fascinated by the sovereign authority of this man who did not just invite them to follow the law of God or the way of salvation, but who said imperiously, 'Follow me!' They had been dazzled, as others had doubtless been scandalized, by this rabbi who did not bother to base himself on the authority of his predecessors or even on that of Moses, but who taught as if his teaching came from the source: 'It has been said . . . but I say' (Matt. 5.21–48). 'They were astonished by his teaching, for he taught as one with authority, and not as the scribes' (Mark 1.22). And the source of this authority was ultimately unveiled when the Risen Christ could say to those who had followed him: 'All power has been given to me on earth and in heaven. Go therefore . . .' (Matt. 28.18f).

This man had spent all his life curing, making

The
Transfiguration.
Fra Angelico.
Museum of San
Marco, Florence.
Photo private
collection

people stand upright, driving out demons, freeing them from evil and death. And people asked where his power came from. Some even suspected that he was acting by Beelzebul, the chief of the demons (Matt. 12.24–27). When God himself snatched Jesus from death, giving him the victory over hatred and sin, all these cures, these resurrections, appeared to be the anticipa-

---

The Kaddish

A very ancient Jewish prayer, the Kaddish was certainly known to Jesus. It has become the traditional prayer that a son recites at the moment of the death of his father.

Raise high and glorify the name of God
Throughout the World He created by His will.
May He build a kingdom in your life,
During your days
And during the life of all the House of Israel.
Soon, and in a time close at hand.
So let us say, Amen.

Let the name of the Holy One
Blessed be He,
Be praised and glorified,
Be exalted, raised up and honoured,
Be magnified and spread.

Though we know He is above all praises
And above all songs of praise
And above all blessings
And all kind words spoken in our world.
Even so, we say, Amen.

Let peace pour from the heavens
With life for us and for all Israel.
Let us say, Amen.

Creator of peace in his high places,
May he create peace for us and for all Israel,
For this we say, Amen.

---

tion, the prefiguration in the life and work of Jesus, of the action of the Father who gives life. Jesus declared the forgiveness of sins (Mark 2.5; Luke 7.48). He welcomed sinners by sharing their meals (Mark 2.16). 'Who does he take himself for?', people asked. In his death he appeared as the one who gives himself to the Father in such filial trust that he can even find forgiveness for his executioners: 'Father, forgive them, for they know not what they do' (Luke 23.34).

Thus at no moment does Jesus become Son of God. He always showed that he was. At the end of his life, in a last prayer, he put everything in the hands of the Father: his life, his ridiculed innocence, his apparently unfulfilled mission (Luke 23.36). But he had lived out this filial relationship from the beginning; the first statement he made was to defend his divine Sonship, to the human kindred by whom he did not want to be imprisoned: 'My child . . . your father and I sought you anxiously . . . Did you not know that I must be in my Father's house?' (Luke 2. 48–49).

The familiarity of his prayer

His prayer was the prayer of his people, that of the psalms and the great blessings. But the disciples had noticed that it was not everyone's prayer, but that of the only Son in an intimate relationship with God his Father. One word described it, which was kept in its Aramaic original: in his prayer Jesus called God Abba. And this expression is precisely the one attested in the prayer of Jesus in Gethsemane, as if to show that it is in the passion of Jesus that the perfect communion of Father and Son, far from slackening, is experienced to the end: 'Abba, Father, all things are possible to thee; remove this cup from me; yet not what I will but what thou will' (Mark 14.36). No one subsequently dared to erase the unaccustomed familiarity of this Abba.

For the disciples of Jesus, to believe him to be

the only Son of God would always be to know that they, too, were authorized to cry 'Abba, Father', with the same boldness as Jesus, and with his Spirit (Rom. 8.15; Gal. 4.6). And yet, when they used the authority of the teaching of their Master to dare to join together in saying Our Father to the one who is primarily the God and Father of Jesus, they remained aware that his relationship continued to be a quite unique one. In his words as reported by the evangelists Jesus always distinguishes between 'My Father' (e.g. Matt. 10.32–33; 12.50) and 'Your Father', the Father of the disciples (Matt. 10.29). It is in the crucifixion and resurrection of Jesus that this twofold Fatherhood finds its fulfilment. There the Father of Jesus becomes fully the Father of his disciples, of his brothers, as Jesus says when he commissions Mary Magdalene to proclaim to them: 'Go to my brethren and say to them that I am ascending to my Father and your Father, to my God and your God' (John 20.17).

Abba

Abba is not used in Jewish prayers as an address to God: to a Jewish mind, it would have been irreverent and therefore unthinkable to call God by this familiar word. It was something new, something unique and unheard of, that Jesus dared to take this step and to speak with God as a child speaks with his father, simply, intimately, securely. There is no doubt, then, that the Abba which Jesus uses to address God reveals the very basis of his communion with God.

Joachim Jeremias, *The Central Message of the New Testament*, SCM Press 1965, p.21

Being Son and knowing it

For Jesus, 'the only Son of God' is therefore much more than a title expressing the veneration of the disciples. For all that one can speak of it with words that describe our human relationships, it denotes primarily the spiritual experience of Jesus himself, his experience of God.

Isaac was everything to Abraham: his only son, his well-beloved child. In Isaac, Abraham recognized himself, his life, his joy, his future (Gen. 20.2). Jesus knows that he is all that to God, by the avowal of God himself: 'You are my Son, the Beloved, my favour rests on you' (Mark 1.11). And it is in this way that God presents him to us: 'This is my well beloved Son, with whom I am well pleased. Listen to him' (Matt. 17.5).

It is the permanent reference to this origin and this proximity which motivates Jesus at every moment and which raises him up again. It is that which sends him and calls him. His awareness of this relationship can burst out in benediction, in jubilant thanksgiving: 'In that same hour he rejoiced in the Holy Spirit and said, "I thank thee, Father, Lord of heaven and earth . . . All things have been delivered to me by my Father; and no one knows who the Son is except the Father, or who the Father is except the Son and any one to whom the Son chooses to reveal him" ' (Luke 20.21–22).

The intuition of this link illuminates the disconcerting boldness of Jesus. The works that he does are not just his own. Another is expressing himself through Jesus (John 7.16; 12.49; 14.10). Jesus is the Word of that other because he is his Son. So what could prove offensive and seem to be a usurpation ('We stone you for no good work but for blasphemy; because you, being a man, make yourself God', John 10.33; cf.5.18), is precisely what should prove illuminating for us: it is because Jesus is God that he can express God.

A difference between the Father and the Son which is the basis for their communion

Because the difference between Jesus and the Father is profound and evocative, it allows a reciprocity between them which St John is particularly fond of stressing. The Son receives from the Father an origin, a *raison d'être* and a Word which he cannot give himself on his own initiative. He is nothing without the Father. At the same time the Father receives from the Son a recognition and an expression which he cannot give himself. He cannot be, without the Son also being in existence. This extraordinary reciprocity ends up in a kind of identification: not an identity which would make it impossible to differentiate between the Son and the Father, but a profound community of condition, will and action. From the point of view of Jesus this union is given, not acquired. It is received, not taken. It is real and effective, not dreamed and imaginary. Moreover the Holy Spirit bears witness to the nature of this identification. Jesus does not claim the Spirit, yet it is given to him. He who does not seek to be identical with the Father has access to the active vitality of the Father. He remains other than the Father, but he is in the closest intimacy with him. Thus the Spirit is common to the Father and the Son. He is the Spirit of the Father and he is the Spirit of the Son. So there is no confusion about this identification. It conjures up and presupposes the difference. While Jesus and the Father in fact have common vitality and action, they remain distinct. They both relate to the Spirit, but in different ways. One is Father, the other is Son. That is irreducible but is the foundation for the most intimate union.

Henri Bourgeois, *Mais il y a Dieu de Jesus-Christ*, Casterman, Tournai 1970

The Church hymns the Son

Hail gladdening Light, of his pure glory poured,
Who is the immortal Father, heavenly, blest,
Holiest of Holies, Jesus Christ our Lord!

Now we are come to the sun's hour of rest,
The lights of evening round us shine.
We hymn the Father, Son, and Holy Spirit
    Divine.

Worthiest art thou at all times to be sung
With undefiled tongue;
Son of our God, giver of life, alone
Therefore in all the world thy glories, Lord, they
    own.

Evening hymn from the earliest centuries of Christianity, translated by John Keble

11   He is God, Born of God

If Jesus truly is the only Son of God, he must always have been so. And the meditation of the church on its Lord, always in the light of Easter and his glorification, is irresistibly orientated on the consideration of its origins. One cannot assign a beginning to the one who in his resurrection, and before that all through his life, appeared so bound up with God that one can in truth give him the name Son, any more than one can assign a beginning to God himself. In the beginning, he was.

Before all ages

That is the solemn proclamation which is the liturgical opening to the Fourth Gospel: 'In the beginning was the Word' (John 1.1). However far we go back in time, and in the time before time, towards God, to the presence of God, utterly intent on him, we already find him, the one who for us was one day to bear the name of Jesus. Focussed on God as he is, all his life, all that he says and does, certainly his death, and his resurrection, point towards God. To such a degree that that defines him, identifies him. It is not only what he does but what he is. He is so Godward, with no barriers, no reticence, no distance, no intermediary, that he is God. 'And the Word was with God and the Word was God.'

For the evangelist these are not abstract expressions, philosophical approximations; this is the very reality of what he has contemplated in Jesus, in flesh and bone. The only Son, 'he who is in the bosom of the Father' (1.18): did not the disciple whom Jesus loved have an intuition of that at the time of the Last Supper, when he

himself was reclining on Jesus' breast (13.2: these are the only two times where this word is used in his Gospel). And Thomas cried out his recognition of Jesus as Lord and God, in a cry of faith, right at the end of the Gospel (20.28), when the apostles, at first unbelieving, fell at the feet of the Risen Jesus to see, in the depth of his wounds, what it is for God to be God.

How do we say who Jesus is in his relationship with the one whom we call our God and whom he calls his Father? Where the Apostles' Creed was content to say that Jesus was the only Son and Lord, the Nicene Creed accumulated convergent affirmations: he is 'eternally begotten of the Father, God from God, Light from Light, true God from true God, of one Being with the Father'.

The church experiences the divinity of Christ

Beyond the words which strive to stammer the divinity of Jesus, there is the recognition by the church of this divinity in its prayer and in its liturgy. People prostrate themselves before Jesus in a gesture of adoration (Matt. 2.2; 8.2; 14.33; 28.17; Luke 24.52; Phil. 2.10). In his martyrdom Stephen turns towards Jesus, just as in his dying Jesus turned towards the Father. It was to Jesus that he could now say, 'Lord Jesus, receive my spirit,' and it was from Jesus that he asked forgiveness for his executioners (Acts 7.59–60; cf. Luke 23.46 and 34). The church prays with Jesus, by him. But it also prays to Jesus. Paul greets the church of God which is in Corinth as 'the community of those who have been sanctified in

Christ Jesus, called to be saints with all those in every place who call upon the name of our Lord Jesus Christ' (I Cor. 1.2). And in the year 110, when a Roman proconsul had to make a report to the emperor Trajan on the activity of the Christians in his province of Bithynia, he was very well aware of what lay at the heart of their life: they meet, he said, 'on a certain day, before sunrise, and they sing a hymn to Christ as to a God' (Pliny the Younger, Letter 96). This *Christo quasi deo* is already a creed in itself.

In the New Testament, the majority of the great texts that the Christians have commented on over twenty centuries to read in them who

Jesus is, are liturgical texts. They include the hymns inserted by Paul into his letters to the Ephesians (1.3–14), the Philippians (2.6–11) and the Colossians (1.15–20). The church hymned its Lord before developing its dogmas. It was first of all in baptism and the eucharist that the Christians had the experience of sharing, in Jesus Christ, in the very life of God. It was then left for theologians like Athanasius (who died in 373), Basil of Caesarea (who died in 379) or Cyril of Alexandria (who died in 444) to explain that the one who has deified us in this way can only be God himself.

A hymn of St Ambrose

O splendour of God's glory bright,
Who bringest forth the light from Light,
O light, of light the fountain spring;
O Day, our days illumining;

Come, very Sun of truth and love
Come in thy radiance from above
And shed the Holy Spirit's ray
On all we think or do or say.

O joyful be the livelong day,
Our thoughts as pure as morning ray,
Our faith like noonday's glowing height,
Our souls undimmed by shades of night.

All praise to God the Father be,
All praise, eternal Son, to thee,
Whom with the Spirit we adore
For ever and for evermore.

The church expresses the divinity of Christ

As if it went without saying, the community of disciples transferred to Jesus many of the titles or expressions which in the Jewish tradition were strictly reserved for God. In inviting the Corin-

thians to call on the name of the Lord Jesus Christ Paul is taking up for Christ with an unprecedented boldness what the prophet Joel said of God himself: 'Whoever calls on the name of the Lord will be saved' (Joel 3.5), and he did so without giving any reason, with a kind of supernatural spontaneity (cf. also Rom. 10.9–13). In the same way, when Paul goes as far as calling Jesus God, *theos*, he does so in passing, without stressing it, as though he were simply taking up some liturgical expression already in use in the communities to which he was writing. To the Romans he speaks of his brethren the Israelites, 'those from whom according to the flesh has come the Christ who is above all, God for ever blessed. Amen' (Rom. 9.5). And he tells Titus, his disciple, to wait for 'the blessed hope and the

---

Jesus as God

The New Testament writers often attest the divinity of Jesus in an indirect way, transferring to him expressions which the Old Testament uses only of God.

That is the case with the title *Lord*: exceptional in Matthew (21.3) and Mark (11.3), very frequent in Luke (7,13; 24,3 etc.) and Paul (Rom. 10.13; I Cor. 1.2; 12.3; II Cor. 1.2; 4.5; I Thess. 1.1); in John, above all in the vocative (13.36), but also of the risen Jesus (20.22; 21.20).

The veneration of the *name* of Jesus: Acts 13.16; Phil. 2.9.

The greeting of his *kingdom*: Matt. 16.28; Luke 22.29–30; 23.42; John 18.36–37; 19.19; I Cor. 15.24–25; Col. 1.13. Ephesians 3.3 speaks in a unique way of the kingdom of Christ and of God.

The contemplation of his *glory*: above all in John (1.14; 2.11; 5.44; 17.5, 22, 24; II Cor. 4.4).

And in the Gospel of John Jesus takes over the 'I am' associated with the revelation of God (John 8.24, 58; 13.19; and the multiple expressions where 'I am' is followed by an attribute. See Ex. 3.14; Isa. 43.10–13.)

The theology of prepositions

The Greek language is rich in prepositions, even if their nuances are blurred in the language of the New Testament. The Fourth Gospel plays on their complementarity to express Jesus in his relationship to the Father.

Jesus comes *from* God
With the Greek *ek*, John 8.42; 16.28.
With *apo*, 3.2; 13.3.
He comes from the presence of (*para*) God: 9.16, 33; 16.27.

Jesus goes *towards* God, he is turned towards him, polarized by him.

With *eis*, 1.18 (Jesus turned towards the being of the Father)
With *pros*: 1.1; 13.3; 16.28; 17.11.

But also God is *with* him (*meta*); 3.2.
He is *in* the Father and the Father is in (*en*) him: 14.10; 17.21

For Jesus these are not successive moments; at each instant, all the time, he is coming from the Father and going towards him. And at the very moment when he is experiencing this double movement which defines the whole of his being, he is dwelling with the Father and in him.

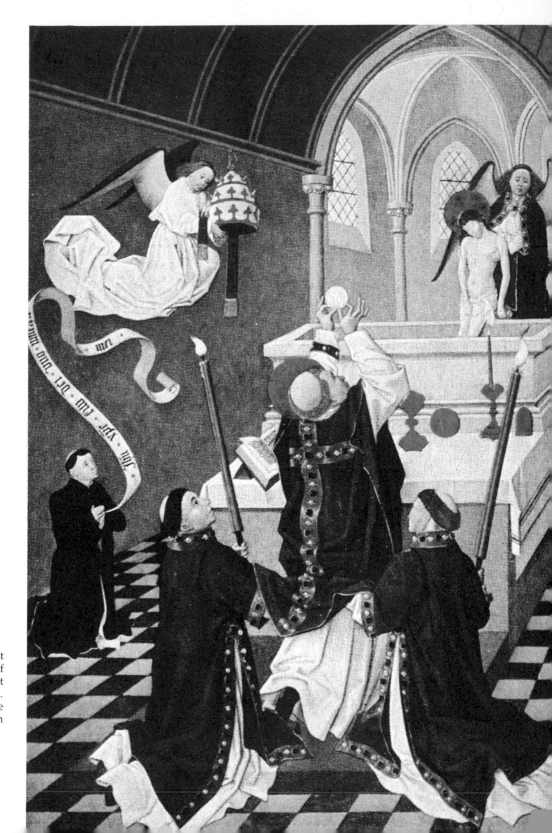

The Mass of St
Gregory. School of
Amiens, about
1440–1450.
Photo private
collection

manifestation of the glory of our great God and Saviour Jesus Christ' (Titus 2.13).

It is with even more solemnity that John constructs his Gospel by including the whole of it between the affirmation of Jesus as God in the prologue (1.1, 18) and Thomas's confession of faith in the presence of the risen Jesus (20.28). That is also the conclusion of his First Letter: 'We know that the Son of God has come and has given us understanding, to know him who is true; and we are in him who is true, in his Son Jesus Christ. This is the true God and eternal life' (I John 5.20).

A council has decided

Though the Church had to convene a council at Nicaea in 325 solemnly to affirm the divinity of Jesus and his eternal unity with the Father, it was not establishing a new doctrine. It now had to defend what it had always believed and experienced. It seemed so much easier to think philosophically in terms of monotheism, faith in the one God, considering that the Father alone is God, and that the Son and the Spirit are only 'super-creatures', certainly the first in creation, but inferior to God and subordinate to him. That was the system of Arius, priest of Alexandria, who for a while seemed to give the whole of Christianity pause. Taken literally, scripture itself did not settle matters. Did not wisdom, in which the church recognized one of the figures of Christ in the Old Testament, itself say in a matter of fact way, 'The Lord created me at the beginning of his work', and 'I was begotten' (Prov. 8.22, 24; cf. Sirach 1.4, 9). And even giving the title *theos*, God, to Christ was no more decisive in the Greek cultural context, where the divine world had somewhat blurred contours.

Hence, as we have already noted, the accumu-

Born of the Father before all ages

The Father and the Son each has the secret of the manner of this birth. If anyone lays upon his personal incapacity his failure to solve the mystery, in spite of the certainty that Father and Son stand to each other in those relations, he will be still more pained at the ignorance to which I confess. I, too, am in the dark, yet I ask no questions.

Listen then to the Unbegotten Father, listen to the Only-begotten Son. Hear his words: 'I and the Father are one'; 'He that hath seen me hath seen the Father also'; 'The Father is in Me and I in the Father'; and 'I went out from the Father', and again, 'Whatsoever the Father hath he hath delivered to the Son'; and again, 'The Son hath life in himself, even as the Father hath in himself. Hear in these words the Son, the Image, the Wisdom, the Power, the Glory of God. Next mark the Holy Ghost proclaiming, 'Who shall declare His generation?' Note the Lord's assurance, 'No one knoweth the Son save the Father, save the Son and he to whom the Son willeth to reveal him.' Penetrate into the mystery, plunge into the darkness which shrouds that birth, where you will be alone with God the Unbegotten and God the Only-begotten. Make your start, continue, persevere. I know that you will not reach the goal, but I shall rejoice at your progress.

Hilary of Poitiers, *De Trintate* II, 9–10

lation by the fathers of Nicaea of convergent expressions, not drawn from scripture, which had to be added to the creed of the church and its baptism. Even the 'consubstantial with the Father', the *homoousios* with its fumbling translations, was not inserted by reason of the clear significance that it could have had beforehand in a philosophical system that enjoyed universal acceptance. Philosophical precisions on nature or substance came only fifty or a hundred years later, with the great theological bishops: Basil the Great (died in 379), Gregory of Nazianzus (died in 394) and in the West Augustine (died in 430). St Ambrose tells us that the word consubstantial was adopted at Nicaea when other assemblies of bishops had thought it suspect only because it was firmly rejected by Arius and his followers.

He is begotten, we are created

The real novelty that was brought out by the Council of Nicaea in connection with these debates on the Christ was the distinction between begotten and created, which it made for the first time; i.e., between the Christ who comes from the Father as Son, emanating from his very being, and the creation which is something that is made by him. God begets his Son and he creates the world. This distinction is decisive for understanding the identity of Jesus and his pre-existence: in the relationship between God and the world the Son is by the side of the God who creates, his Word, as eternal as he is. It is only as man, in the incarnation, that he becomes the head of creation, to bring the divine plan to fulfilment and to advance it towards God. It is as firstborn among the dead that he appears as the firstborn of all creation (Col. 1.15,18).

This distinction between begotten and created is also basic for an understanding of creation. Contrary to all the pantheisms, in which everything is God because the world is an emanation of God, God dispersed through all things, as a result of the clarification made at Nicaea the world takes on a real otherness in the face of God. It has its consistency, its own norms, its autonomy. There can be scientific laws, and what Vatican II will call 'an autonomy of earthly values'. Desacralized, in the sense that it is not God, the world can become the object of science. It escapes magic. One might suppose that the extraordinary wealth of scientific knowledge in the Western world is also in part a fruit of this distinction made by the Council of Nicaea.

God as Son

What was really at stake in these first reflections of the church on the identity of Jesus was the perception that Sonship is not in itself a matter of being inferior. 'Coming from' . . . 'going to' express a relationship. And for Christ this is not a relationship added to what he is, like the relationships that we can acquire. This relationship of origin and vocation (the Son comes from the Father and goes towards the Father) constitutes him and is his very being. At the time when a technical form of theology was being constructed, St Thomas Aquinas spoke in connection with the divine Persons of 'subsistent relationships'.

The Father, the one to whom the New Testament continues to give the name of God, is also relational. If there is no Son without the Father, there is no Father without the Son either. And the Spirit is the Spirit of the Father and the Son. This interdependence is not inferiority but sharing and communion.

Hence the divinity of Jesus does not fall short in any way of that of the Father. On the contrary, it reveals the true nature of the Godhead, which is love and sharing. Already in the New Testament, the confession of faith in Jesus is expressed as a doubling of faith in God. So we have sorts of confessions of faith with two terms: 'For us there is one God, the Father, from whom are all things and for whom we exist, and one Lord, Jesus Christ, through whom are all things and through whom we exist' (I Cor. 8.6; cf. also Eph. 4.6; I Tim. 2.5; John 17.3). This is the very origin, the matrix, of our baptismal creed and its trinitarian structure. The three affirmations of faith are not concurrent but convergent. God is one, and this oneness is the oneness of love.

So we can see why there will always be ambiguity in affirming the divinity of Jesus, his nature, his divine condition, without at the same time relating it to the Father. To speak of his divinity without mentioning his Sonship is to expose oneself to making it a kind of personal power, absolute omnipotence, which in addition is apparently incompatible with his humanity.

Jesus is God, but he is God *qua* Son. He is God in the form of a son.

That does not mean that he is inferior. For at the same time we discover that the Father is God, not in the imprisonment of a closed divine nature: he is God after the manner of a father. Being Father is his way of expressing that he is God, sharing from eternity his very being with the Son and the Spirit, so that in a flood of free grace, this sharing can extend to us. We are created and not begotten, but we have been created, chosen, loved, so that one day we may be gathered together in the one who has been begotten, the Son in whom the Father is well pleased. Jesus is God, Son of God, that we might become children of God.

Becoming God

But give me now your best attention, I pray you, for I wish to go back to the fountain of life, and to view the fountain that gushes with healing. The Father of immortality sent the immortal Son and Word into the world, who came to man in order to wash him with water and the Spirit; and he, begetting us again to incorruption of soul and body, breathed into us the breath of life and endued us with an incorruptible panoply. If, therefore, man has become immortal, he will also be God. And if he is made God by water and the Holy Spirit after the regeneration of the laver he is found to be also joint heir with Christ after the resurrection from the dead.

Wherefore I preach to this effect: Come all ye kindreds of the nations, to the immortality of the baptism . . . This is the water in conjunction with the spirit, by which paradise is watered, by which the earth is enriched, by which plants grow, by which animals multiply and (to sum up the whole in a single word) by which man is begotten again and endued with life, in which also Christ was baptized and in which the Spirit descended in the form of a dove.

He who comes down in faith to the laver of regeneration and renounces the devil and joins himself to Christ, who denies the enemy and makes the confession that Christ is God; who puts off the bondage and puts on the adoption – he comes up from the baptism brilliant as the sun, flashing forth the beams of righteousness, and which is indeed the chief thing, he returns a son of God and joint-heir with Christ.

Discourse on the Holy Theophany, attributed to Hippolytus of Rome, *Ante-Nicene Fathers* Vol. V, p.237

12 All is by Him and for Him

Jesus is not simply in the middle of our creed. He is its centre. Because he is the centre of the world and history. He is 'the focal point of the desires of history and civilization, the centre of mankind, · the joy of all hearts and the fulfilment of all aspirations' (Vatican II, *Gaudium et Spes*, no.45, 2).

The pole of history

The Word of God, through whom all things were made, was made flesh, so that as a perfect man he could save all men and sum up all things in himself. The Lord is the goal of human history, the focal point of the desires of history and civilization, the centre of mankind, the joy of all hearts, and the fulfilment of all aspirations. It is he whom the Father raised from the dead, exalted and placed at his right hand, constituting him judge of the living and the dead. Animated and drawn towards the consummation of his-tory which fully corresponds to the plan of his love: 'to unite all things in him, things in heaven and things on earth' (Eph. 1.10).

The Lord himself said: 'Behold, I am coming soon, bringing my recompense, to repay every one for what he has done. I am the alpha and the omega, the first and the last, the beginning and the end' (Rev. 22.12–13).

Vatican II, *Gaudium et Spes*, 45.2–3

Everything towards him

On the tympana of Romanesque churches and on the cupolas of Byzantine basilicas Christ in majesty opens his arms to welcome and bless the entire universe. He is the Pantocrator. 'All power has been given to me in heaven and on earth' (Matt. 28.19). For the disciple who recognizes his divinity, that is to say his original relationship of unity with the Father, it appears that this universal power, inaugurated in its fullness in his resurrection, has its roots in his very being as only Son from all ages with the Father. When we arrive, with the risen Christ, at the end of our history, we discover with . . . that he can only be its origin, its first intention. As St Maximus the Confessor wrote: It is the eyes turned towards him that God has called into existence.

The originality of Christianity, hymned in the creed before being stammered by the theologians, is to believe that our history, which comes from God and goes towards him, finds its dynamic and its significance in the existence of Jesus, the Son *par excellence*, the one in whom all comes from God and goes towards him. Jesus, who appeared at a lowly point of history, in an unimportant country on the planet Earth, is himself the author by whom the worlds are organized. That is because he is the perfect incarnation of what God has dreamed of since the beginning, of that for which he has called all things from non-being to being: the well-beloved Son, in his life, his death and his resurrection, he is the man after God's heart: he is the success of the world.

Everything was created with a view to the resurrection

The mystery of the incarnation of the Word contains in itself the meaning of all the symbols and all the enigmas of scripture, and the hidden sense of all creation that can be perceived and understood. But he who knows the mysteries of the cross and the tomb also knows the essential reasons of all things. Finally, he who penetrates further and finds himself initiated into the mystery of the resurrection learns the end for which God created all things in the beginning.

Maximus the Confessor (died 662), *Gnostic Centuries* I.66

The wisdom that sits by the throne

O God of my fathers and Lord of mercy,
who hast made all things by thy word,
and by thy wisdom has formed man,
to have dominion over the creatures thou hast
    made,
and rule the world in holiness and
    righteousness,
and pronounce judgment in uprightness of soul,
give me the wisdom that sits by thy throne,
and do not reject me from among your servants.

With thee is wisdom, who knows thy works
and was present when thou didst make the
    world,
and who understands what is pleasing in thy
    sight
and what is right according to thy
    commandments.

Prayer of Solomon, Wisdom 9. 1–4, 9–10

The Father's wisdom

This Christocentricity, which puts Christ at the centre of the universe just as the sun stands at the beginning and the centre of our solar system, is prefigured in the Old Testament. The Jewish tradition already celebrates Wisdom, the emanation of the power of God, the pure radiance of the glory of the Almighty, whose throne it shares (Wisdom 7.25; 9.4). Begotten from the beginning wisdom is beside God as his master craftsman of creation (Prov. 8). Wisdom, and this theme was already familiar throughout the Greek world, is as it were God's intuition on the world.

For a Christian like the author of the Epistle to the Colossians it became evident that it was Jesus who was God's intuition on the world, from the beginning. So Paul could hymn Christ as his forebears hymned wisdom: 'He is the image of the invisible God, the firstborn of all creation' (Col. 1.15–20). The wisdom which explains the origin and evolution of the worlds is Christ: 'He is before all things . . . that in everything he might be preeminent. For in him all the fullness of God was pleased to dwell.' This hymn in the Letter to the Colossians is built up entirely on two words: all (the universe), and him (Christ). All is by him, for him, in him. Because in the end all has been reconciled by him and for him, by his cross, we can see that 'in him all things are created, in heaven and on earth, visible and invisible, whether thrones or dominations or

Christ on the Cross. Twelfth-century mosaic from the church of St Clement, Rome. Photo private collection

62

Brought into being before the ages

The Lord created me at the beginning of his
    work,
the first of his acts of old.
Ages ago I was set up,
at the first, before the beginning of earth.

When there were no depths I was brought forth,
when there were no springs abounding with
    water.
Before the mountains had been shaped,
before the hills I was brought forth;
before he had made the earth with its fields;
or the first of the dust of the world.
When he had established the heavens, I was
    there,
when he drew a circle on the face of the deep,
when he made firm the skies above,
when he established the fountains of the deep.
When he assigned to the sea its limit,
so that the waters might not transgress his
    command;
when he marked out the foundations of the
    earth,
then I was beside him, like a master workman;
and I was daily his delight,
rejoicing before him always,
rejoicing in his inhabited world
and delighting in the sons of men.

Proverbs 8. 22–31

The Church hymns the firstborn

He is the image of the invisible God,
the firstborn of all creation;
for in him all things were created,
in heaven and on earth,
visible and invisible,
whether thrones or dominations
or principalities or authorities,
all things were created through him and for him.

He is before all things,
and in him all things hold together.

He is the head of the body, the church;
he is the beginning;
the firstborn from the dead,
that in everything he might be preeminent.

For in him the fullness of God
was pleased to dwell,
and through him to reconcile to himself all
    things,
whether on earth or in heaven,
making peace by the blood of his cross.

Colossians 1.15–20

principalities or authorities – all things were created through him and for him. He is before all things and in him all things hold together' (Col. 1.16f).

Alpha and omega

In front of the paschal candle we sing that the risen Christ is the alpha and omega of our history. It is because he is the goal, the omega on which all converges, that we recognize that he is the origin, the alpha, in whom all was already willed, foreseen and loved: 'He chose us in him before the foundation of the world, with the great plan, the purpose which he set forth in Christ as a plan for the fullness of time, to unite all things to him, things in heaven and things on earth' (Eph. 1.4, 9–10). To understand the universe and that to which humankind is called we must look at the risen Christ in whom the millennia of grace and the Spirit finally fashioned the perfect image and likeness of the Creator.

Adam was only a sketch; in Jesus the world is fulfilled, all is accomplished, because God has at last been totally expressed and totally given. In his passion and his resurrection Jesus is the image of the invisible God (Col. 1.15). 'In many and various ways God spoke of old to our fathers by the prophets; but in these last days he has spoken to us by a Son, whom he had appointed the heir of all things, through whom also he created the world. He reflects the glory of God and bears the very stamp of his nature, upholding the universe by his word of power' (Heb. 1.1–3).

In the beginning he is the Word

He who was given to us in the last days thus seems to be bound up with the creation of the worlds. Because he is the fulfilment of history he is its origin. In the beginning was the Word, sings the Prologue of the Gospel of John. Not as an abstract philosophy but as the fruit of the contemplation of the disciple and his community: no one has seen God at any time, but the only Son, the one who in his life, death and resurrection appears ceaselessly close to the Father's heart, he has made him known (see John 1.18). If we have seen this link all through the life of Jesus we can say that we have seen his glory, which is itself the original bond of the Son with the Father through all ages (1.14). All his life for us is light, because it speaks of the Father throughout. Everything in Jesus, the least word, the least gesture, speaks. Not only because he perfectly matches what he says, but because he is totally transparent to the one to whom he points and whom he reveals, the Father. He is God's word. He is God who speaks.

So the life of Jesus, in which this word takes form, in an enchantment which contradicts all our ethereal ideas about God, illuminates the destiny of man and the history of the world for us. Since God's goal, objective, dream is that in Jesus all should become his children (John 1.12), we must see at the beginning of all things this

well-beloved Son in whom all are invited to find life and light (1.4). He is the effective and creative word brought forth by God at the beginning so that in the mists and even the shadows of our history a response to his love can one day be articulated. At the beginning the word of God is uttered as a call ('Adam, where are you?', Gen. 3.9) so that the word of man, that of the Son, may one day take form down the generations: 'Here I am, come to do your will' (Heb. 10.9). Everything has been created and willed for that. Jesus is the perfect gift of the Father and he is our sole response. That is why, at the end of a kind of retrospective rereading of our history in the light of the existence of Jesus, we can finally say what was there at the beginning: at the beginning of everything there is him, Jesus, the word of the Father. From the beginning he is with God, and all is directed towards him. 'All things were made through him, and without him was not anything made that was made' (John 1.3). He is not only there at the beginning; he is the beginning (Col. 1.18; Rev. 22.13).

Jesus, the genesis of the world

In this way, then, in the light of the Easter Christ, Christians can reread the book of origins. Christ is the key to Genesis. When in the beginning God created heaven and earth, was not this beginning, this principle, in whom all was chosen, willed and loved, already Christ himself? It is by his Word that God calls all things into being. 'God said . . . And it was so . . . And God saw that it was good.' When God says, 'Let us make man in our image according to our likeness' (Gen. 1.26), with this strange plural he has Jesus at the back of his mind, the image of the invisible God.

The salvation in Jesus Christ of which we shall be speaking as the creed goes on will not, then, be a second divine plan, a correction added to the original plan to cope with the failure of creation and sin. As the French bishops said at Lourdes in 1968, 'There are not two successive divine plans, one of creation and the other of redemption. There is only one divine plan. God calls all men to the communion of life in his Son. The creation is the first stage of the covenant. Christ is the truth of Creation.'

So all creation (and the universe in its material nature) is involved with Christ and polarized by him. Because all things are created in Christ and for him, it is the whole universe, the cosmos, which is caught up, recapitulated, saved in Jesus Christ. The world, which only exists with a view to Christ, finds its justification in him. 'For the creation waits with eager longing for the revelation of the Son of God . . . We know that the whole creation has been groaning in travail together until now' (Rom. 8.19, 22). The universe is there for humanity. Humanity is made for filial love in Jesus Christ. And Christ lives only for the Father. Thus the Spirit of Jesus, the Spirit in which he is one with the Father, is at work in the universe from the very beginning (Gen. 1.2) in a universal polarization towards the love of the Trinity.

By him, with him and in him

Christian reflection on the world and humanity is thus focussed on seeing everything in the light of the incarnate Word, in whom everything finds its cohesion and its goal. 'The church . . . believes that the key, the centre and the purpose of the whole of man's history is to be found in its Lord and Master' (*Gaudium et Spes*, 10.2). 'In reality it is only in the mystery of the Word made flesh that the mystery of man truly becomes clear' (Ibid., 22).

So Christ is God's way towards humankind and our way towards God. 'No one comes to the Father but by me' (John 14.6). This 'by' (Greek *dia*) is characteristic of the Son. He is the one mediator between God and man (I Tim. 2.5). Because he is the mediator in our prayer and our return to the Father we discover that from the beginning he is the mediator of all created existence and every outpouring of the love of the Father. It is this mediation that we confess in our creed. St Paul already proclaimed: 'There is only God, the Father, from whom are all things and for whom we exist, and one Lord, Jesus Christ, through whom are all things and through whom we exist' (I Cor. 8.6). In this small Pauline creed there is no verb, only prepositions ('From whom, for whom, through whom') so we could also expand the last words to read: 'Through whom all things exist and through whom we go towards the Father'.

In the Church, every eucharistic prayer ends with this universal recapitulation in Jesus Christ, in which humanity and creation find themselves grasped to be presented to God the Father: 'By him, with him, and in him, to you, God the Father Almighty, in the unity of the Holy Spirit, be all honour and glory world without end.'

The Lord of the universe

Glorious Lord Christ:
the divine influence secretly diffused and active in the depths of matter, and the dazzling centre where all the innumerable fibres of the manifold meet; power as implacable as the world and as warm as life; you whose forehead is of the whiteness of snow, whose eyes are of fire, and whose feet are brighter than molten gold; you whose hands imprison the stars; you who are the first and the last, the living and the dead and the risen again; you who gather into your exuberant unity every beauty, every affinity, every energy, every mode of existence; it is you to whom my being cried out with desire as vast as the universe, 'In truth you are my Lord and my God'.

Pierre Teilhard de Chardin, 'The Mass on the World', *Hymn of the Universe*, Fount Paperbacks 1977, p.33

13 For Us and for Our Salvation

'Us men': at the heart of the Creed, this is where we break in: we and our preoccupations, our affairs, our salvation. It might even seem as if we were shifting something from beside God and this Son by whom and for whom all has been made: 'For us men and for our salvation he came down from heaven.' Here God mobilizes himself. The eternal enters time. The Word becomes history, human history. For you, for me. 'From now on,' wrote François Mauriac, in every human destiny there will be this God lying in wait.'

God saves from all eternity

And this expectation of God goes back to the beginning. Our origin is God's hope, God's desire. From eternity God has expected something of humanity, God has been waiting for us, as a wife expects her child, as a people expects its messiah. God chose our fathers: for Paul preaching the history of salvation to his Jewish brothers, this divine action is the beginning of everything (Acts 13.17). In the beginning God loved and God chose. The creation itself was covenant, communion of will, primordial salvation, even more original than sin. All history is the deployment of this salvation. God gives growth and God guides. God gives, restores and pardons. God brings out, raises up, indeed raises to new life (see Acts 13.17–23), in a kind of escalation, a raising of the stakes, in which Jesus is the culminating point. 'Of his fullness we have all received and grace for grace' (John 1.16).

God brings forth

In the memory of Israel the events of the exodus are constantly meditated upon as the fundamental revelation of the God who saves. In snatching his people from forced labour in the slavery of Egypt God comes to find them, to win them, to bind them to himself: 'We were Pharaoh's slaves in Egypt; and the Lord brought us out of Egypt with a mighty hand; and the Lord showed signs and wonders, great and grievous, against Egypt and against Pharaoh and all his household, before our eyes; and he brought us out from there, that he might bring us in and give us the land which he swore to give to our fathers' (Deut. 6.21–23). 'It is because the Lord loves you, and is keeping the oath which he swore to your fathers, that the Lord has brought you out with a mighty hand, and redeemed you from the house of bondage, from the hand of Pharaoh king of Egypt. Know therefore that the Lord your God is God, the true God . . .' (Deut. 7.8–9). The exodus is God's liberation and God's guidance. In this action, the foundation of the people and his history, he expresses himself and he binds himself. 'Is there on earth a nation like Israel your people, this people that God has redeemed to make his people?' (II Sam. 17.23). From now on the covenant is sealed. God is the God of Israel, our God, and Israel is God's people. God is God 'for us and for our salvation'.

The hope of our fathers

When in their eucharistic prayer Christians hymn the God who saves, they remember the pedagogy of God who, throughout the history of Israel, renews his covenant offer so as to accustom human beings to live his life: 'Again and again you offered a covenant to man, and

66

through the prophets taught him to hope for salvation' (Eucharistic Prayer IV). The parables of Jesus express this obstinacy of the Father, who never takes account of our non-responses and our refusals. The master so loves his vineyard that he sends successively to it all his servants, the prophets, at the risk of seeing them ill-treated and massacred (Matt. 12.1–5). The Master so loves his Son, the ultimate argument of his

---

Accustoming man to receive God

It is indeed the Word of God who dwelt in man, and became the Son of man, that he might accustom man to receive God, and God to dwell in man, according to the good pleasure of the Father.

On this account, therefore, the Lord himself, who is Immanuel from the Virgin, is the sign of our salvation, since it was the Lord himself who saved them, because they could not be saved by their own instrumentality; and therefore, when Paul sets forth human infirmity, he says: 'For I know that no good thing dwells in my flesh', showing that the 'good thing' of our salvation is not from us, but from God. And again he says, 'Wretched man that I am, who shall deliver me from the body of this death?' Then he introduces the deliverer, saying 'The grace of Jesus Christ our Lord'. Isaiah declares this also: 'Be strengthened, hands that hang down and feeble knees; be encouraged, feeble minds; be comforted, fear not; behold our God has given judgment with retribution, and shall recompense: He will come himself and will save us.' Here we see that we must be saved not by ourselves, but by the help of God.

Irenaeus, *Against the Heresies* III. 20.3

---

fatherly heart, that he sent him as an irrevocable proof of his desire to bind himself to us: 'Father you so loved the world that in the fullness of time you sent your only Son to be our Saviour' (Eucharistic Prayer IV, cf. Mark 12.6; John 3.16).

Taking Mary's son in his arms, the old man Simeon was aware of at last grasping the promise made to Israel and the salvation of the whole world: 'My eyes have seen thy salvation' (Luke 3.40). The hope of so many generations of patriarchs, sages and prophets finds its justification in him. 'Abraham your father rejoiced to see my day; he saw it and was transported with joy' (John 8.56). But this long expectation, this hope extending over thousands of years, is primarily that of God himself from the beginning, a God in search of humankind: 'Where are you?' (Gen. 3.9). It is a God looking for a partner, an echo, a filial acceptance.

Sinners from the beginning

Christians confess that sin is original. Not because it is part of human nature but as a simple limit: God himself attests to his creation 'that it was very good' (Gen. 1.31). Nor to pretend that sin commands and explains the history of salvation: in the beginning there was not darkness, but light; in the beginning was the Word. The Christ is more original than all our refusals.

But God who, from all eternity, wants to make us his children and who in every generation brushes aside our refusals, persists in his offer of covenant and communion even when we are sinners (Rom. 5.8). Our solidarity in Jesus Christ in whom we have all been willed, created and loved, and in whom we are expected, reveals and denounces an opposite solidarity, that which binds us and imprisons us in the original refusal, that of Adam. 'But the free gift is not like the trespass. For if many died through one man's trespass, much more have the grace of God and the free gift in the grace of that one man Jesus Christ abounded for many' (Rom. 5.15).

67

However, it is not Adam who illuminates and explains our salvation in Jesus Christ. It is the other way round: the Christ, the last Adam, the true man, with a view to whom everything was conceived, binds us together at this point so that the least refusal, from the beginning, could not but be contagious. It is the perspective of Christ that we are in solidarity with Adam, 'For God has consigned all men to disobedience, that he may have mercy upon all' (Rom. 11.329).

Adam, 'the figure of him who was to come' (Rom. 5.14), was only the outline, too quickly disfigured. Christ is the image of the invisible God, the firstborn of all creation (Col. 1.15). In this history of love between God and man he incarnates the faithfulness of God, utterly shown in his Son, and finally expresses the free response of humanity. 'For all the promises of God find their Yes in him. That is why we utter the Amen through him, to the glory of God' (II Cor. 1.20).

The paradoxes of salvation

He was made flesh
that we might be made to possess the Spirit.
He was humiliated in goodness
to raise us up.
He came from him
to lead us to him.
He appeared visibly to our eyes
to show us that which is invisible.

He endured blows
to heal us.
He sustained outrage and mockery
to deliver us from eternal opprobrium.
He died
to give us life.

Gregory the Great (died 604), *Homilies on Ezekiel* II.4.20

Becoming sons in the Son

So Christ does not wrest our salvation from a vengeful and legalistic God who from the beginning of time has looked for recompense for the whole accumulation of sin. The God who has created everything in his Son is the one who welcomes us and forgives us in this same Son: 'For God was in Christ reconciling the world to himself' (II Cor. 5.19). All the attempts of Christian theology to express this salvation in human words (justification, redemption, expiation, satisfaction, liberation, reconciliation) stammer in their attempt to express this divine gesture which comes to take hold of us at the very heart of our imprisonment as sinners.

For us this salvation is not only restoration, a return to primordial paradise: Adam did not share in the life of God as we are invited to do in Jesus Christ. This salvation is not a simple judicial action, arbitration, compensation or amnesty by which God, through the intervention of his Son, agreed to consider us just without our being really changed. Salvation is real participation in the life which God offers, which is none other than participation in the life of the Trinity: being united with Jesus to allow oneself to be loved by the Father in the illumination of the Holy Spirit. The Greek Fathers speak here of divinization. 'The Word of God was made man, he who is the Son of God was made son of man that man might become the son of God, in communion with the Word of God and by receiving adoption (Irenaeus, *Against the Heresies* III. 19.1). Not that human beings cease to be human, but because each one of us, however

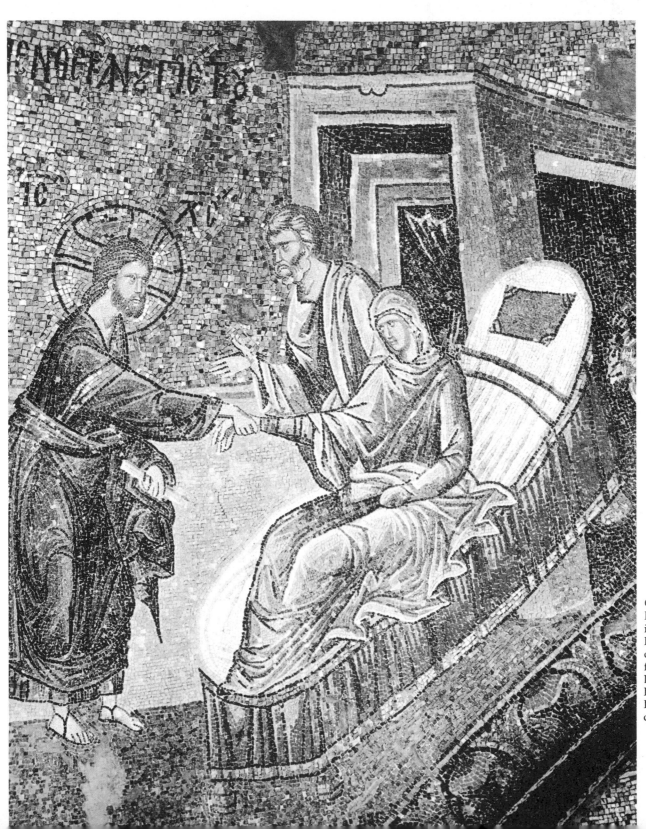

Christ heals
Peter's Mother-
in-Law.
Fourteenth-
century mosaic
from Kahriye
Djami,
Istanbul.
Photo private
collection

Truth has sprung up from the earth, and justice has come down from heaven

Awaken, O man; God has been made man for you. Awaken, you who sleep, rise from the dead and Christ will give you light. For you, I repeat, God has been made man. You would be dead for eternity had he not been born in time. You would never have been freed from sinful flesh had he not taken the likeness of sin. You would be the victim of misery without end had he not shown you this mercy. You would not have rediscovered life had he not shared in your death. You would have succumbed had he not come to your aid. You would have perished had he not come.

Let us celebrate in joy the advent of our salvation and our redemption. Let us celebrate the festival in which, coming from the great day of eternity, a great eternal day introduces itself into our temporal day, short as it is. God has made us righteous by faith, so let us be at peace with God, because justice and peace have kissed each other. By our Lord Jesus Christ, for Truth has sprung up from the earth. It is he who opens up to us access to the world of grace in which we are established, and our pride is to have a share in the glory of God. Paul does not say to our glory but to the glory of God, because justice has not come forth from us but has come down from heaven. So let him who seeks his glory glory not in himself but in the Lord.

Augustine, *Sermon 185* for Christmas

sinful, bears within himself or herself as his or her most profound identity the imprint of our Creator and the desire of our God. Hence to be saved is much more than to cease being a sinner. It is finally to accede to this desire which faith tells us, in God, is sufficiently strong to come to the end of our evasions and our refusals; it is what we call the grace of God, that is to say, the fascination of his grace transforming our life.

Do not forget your birth

Dearly beloved, we must give thanks to God the Father, by his Son, in the Holy Spirit; with the great mercy with which he has loved us, he has taken pity on us, and when we were dead as a result of our sins he revived us with Christ that in him we might be a new creation, a new work of his hands.

So let us put off the old man with his actions, and since we are allowed to participate in the birth of Christ, let us renounce our carnal conduct.

Christian, be aware of your dignity. Since you now participate in the divine nature, do not become degenerate by returning to the corruption of your past life. Remember the leader to whom you belong and the body of which you are a member. Remember that you have been snatched from the power of darkness to be transferred into the light and kingdom of God.

Leo the Great, *Sermons for Christmas* 1.3

→

When God comes down from heaven

God has sent his Son Jesus to be the hope and defence of the weak, the outcast and the oppressed. Jesus, too, rebuked his disciples when they were harsh to children; attached importance to the humble gesture of the prostitute; saved from lynching the wife who had deceived her husband; sat at table with people of bad reputation like the tax collectors; and even chose Matthew, one of them, to become an apostle. In an attitude of forgiveness and mercy he has left the ninety-nine sheep which were saved to go in search of the one which was lost.

The church must follow the example of Christ. It has no right to exclude anyone and must offer to everyone, both great and small, the means of salvation which it has received from Christ. But its choices and its preferences are for the weak and the oppressed. It cannot remain insensitive to the despoiling of the Indian who is driven from his land or to the destruction of his culture. It cannot close its eyes to the situation of insecurity experienced by ordinary people, to famine among the poor and malnutrition among children. It cannot ignore those without roots, the migrants looking for new opportunities, who find shelter only under the bridges, or who cram into the shanty-towns. Christ makes himself present and visible in these persons. To ill-treat them is to ill-treat Christ.

Pastoral communication to the people of God from the bishops of Brazil, 25 October 1976

Every man and the whole man

Such a salvation necessarily affects our humanity in every dimension. It concerns everyone, everyone called by his or her name, but also human beings in their relationships, their solidarities, human beings called to form a people, a body, to make a church with all those who are called. It recreates us human beings in our intelligence, in our understanding of God, in our heart, our emotions, but also in our body, our presence in the world and in history. What Vatican II called 'the full ideal which God has set for man' (*Gaudium et Spes* 11.1) is the impact of the resurrection of Jesus on everything that makes human beings human.

He descended

Thus, bringing his plan of a covenant, his intention of communion to full term, God abolishes all distance: that which we might imagine spontaneously between the Creator and his creation, and that which we constantly add by our refusals to love. God takes the initiative in bridging this distancing and moving towards us. He came down from heaven, we confess of the Son in his incarnation. The important thing is that we do not see any kind of condescension: in coming to us and his Son, God does not demean himself (he does not leave heaven). His love does not look down on us from on high, his pity does not humiliate us. And he himself is not changed by us. For us, true love is never demeaning. All the more reason that this should be so for God, the one for whom to be God is to love. In this proximity to Christ who makes himself our neighbour, everyone's neighbour (see Luke 10.36), we shall finally know that God is God; we shall finally see what it is to be God.

14   He Took Flesh and was Made Man

By the Holy Spirit

In the beginning there was the Spirit. Our creed has not yet spoken of him, but without the Spirit, who would proclaim the creed? (see I Cor. 12.3). At Pentecost, he is at the beginning of the Church. At the Annunciation he is at the beginning of the earthly life of Jesus. But if it is true that the intention of the Father Creator in fashioning the world was that the beloved Son might one day assume a body there, his Spirit must have been at work from the beginning: we see him brooding on the primordial chaos (Gen. 1.2) so that one day love can germinate there, and we recognize his breath in the hope of the prophets, intent on the coming of the Messiah of the Lord.

The Spirit in whom all that comes from God is born, even today, is thus at the origin of the incarnation of the only Son. 'The Holy Spirit will come upon you and the power of the Most High will overshadow you,' were the words that Mary heard (Luke 1.35). It is also true that at the beginning of everything there is the Word, the Word of God, and God's desire to plant it among us from the beginning; there is in God this desire to love. In the beginning there is the Spirit.

Of the Virgin Mary

That is why the coming of Jesus was both ardently expected and totally unhoped for. Jesus, of the race of David, is the fruit of the hope of the prophets and the faith of Mary. Matthew and Luke gives us his genealogy. He was not a meteor fallen from heaven. 'When the earth opens and brings forth its Redeemer', runs the Advent liturgy, Jesus took flesh of the Virgin Mary: he is born of her and not just in her. And Joseph, son of David, in accepting Jesus as his son, could legally inscribe him in the royal line (Matt. 1.21).

Mary represents all humanity awaiting a saviour, and she sums up in herself the faith of the church: to say Jesus is son of Mary is to say that he is fully man, and to proclaim Mary mother of God is to recognize Jesus as being truly God.

Later, the councils will have to affirm the humanity of Jesus. The mention of Mary in the creed of the first communities already bears witness to the authenticity of this humanity. In the church, down through the centuries, Marian devotion regularly attests in the liturgy and in prayer what the councils solemnly proclaimed: the humanity of Jesus is drawn from ours. A mother taught him to speak and pray. She ensures that Jesus has roots in the history of his people: it is in this people and in its traditions, in its adoration of the one God, in his pilgrimages and his benedictions, that Jesus has become the man that he is.

However, human history in itself cannot give birth to its saviour. The spiritual energies of the universe awaiting its fulfilment, all the quests for wisdom by a humanity which dreams of conquering death, the millennial hope of a whole people which knows that God keeps his promises, all that cannot in itself engender Christ. History by itself does not bring forth God. All this accumulated faith can only open itself up, when the moment comes, to the absolutely free

Theotokos

Very early on in the liturgy and in the prayer of the Church Mary was invoked as Mother of God, Theotokos. This happens in a Greek antiphon which may go back to the third century: 'We take refuge under the protection of your mercy, Mother of God: do not reject our prayers in need, but deliver us from danger, you who alone are pure and blessed.'

In the fourth century Nestorius, Patriarch of Constantinople, reproached Christians for using this title. 'Does God have a mother?' He was condemned by the Council of Ephesus in 431.

Certainly Mary is not the mother of God the Father, nor mother of the divinity of Jesus, but she is mother of Jesus who is truly God. Jesus, God and man, is one person. Mary is not only mother of the man who would come to being in Jesus. She did not give birth to the eternal Person of the Son, the Word of God, but she exercised true motherhood towards him by giving birth to him according to his humanity. It is in this sense that Cyril of Alexandria could proclaim: Anyone who does not confess that Emmanuel is truly God and that for this reason the Holy Virgin is Mother of God (for she gave birth to the Word of God made flesh according to the flesh), let him be anathema!

---

gift of God. For that to happen, the spark of the Spirit is needed.

To hymn Jesus as being conceived by the Holy Spirit is to proclaim that he is a new creation. It is to proclaim that when he takes a body today in our history, through evangelization, in catechesis or by the sacraments, he is always the free gift of God. It is just as in the eucharist, where the bread does not become the body of Jesus Christ without the invocation of the Holy Spirit: 'Father, may this Holy Spirit sanctify these offerings. Let them become the body and blood of Jesus Christ our Lord . . .' (Eucharistic Prayer IV).

When God comes to us in Jesus his Son, it is always he who has the initiative. 'He came down from heaven' does not signify a condescension on the part of God or an abdication of the divinity the Son might have, but it is he who takes the first step. All the towers of Babel crumble in one way or another. Every human striving to climb up towards God, by means of philosophical reflection, moral asceticism and merit, or even spiritual elevation, needs to be converted, i.e.

turned back. The desire for the Spirit to enter into us is a matter of welcoming the free grace of God which, in Jesus, takes shape in our history.

In a history

The creed says nothing of the history of Jesus. From the nativity it jumps to the passion. Is this a desire not to dwell on what was never challenged, a conviction that the essential events took place at Easter? But for us a human being means having a history. One is born human, that is true. But one also becomes human through growth, education, opening oneself to others in a complex of relationships. And the evangelists, while discreet about the childhood of Jesus, are keen to bear witness to his actions during all the time that he spent with his disciples, 'from the baptism of John to the day when he was taken up' (Acts 1.21). The catechesis of the first communities, before the Gospels were even written, was fond of summing up the career of Jesus in several phrases: 'How God anointed Jesus of Nazareth with the Holy Spirit and with power; how he went about doing good and healing all

The Church hymns Mary Mother of God

We hail thee, Mary, Mother of God, sacred treasure of the whole universe, star who never sets, crown of virginity, sceptre of the orthodox faith, indestructible temple, dwelling of the incommensurable, Mother and Virgin, for the sake of him who is called blessed in the holy gospels, him who comes in the name of the Lord.

We hail thee, thou who didst contain in thy virginal womb him whom the heavens could not contain; thee by whom the Trinity is glorified and adored throughout the earth; through whom heaven exults; by whom the angels and archangels are made to rejoice; by whom the demons are put to rout; by whom the tempter fell from heaven; by whom the humiliated creature is raised to heaven; by whom the whole world in the captivity of idolatry has come to the knowledge of the truth; by whom holy baptism is given to those who believe, with the oil of gladness; by whom all churches have been founded all over the earth; by whom the pagan nations have been led to conversion.

What more shall I say? It is by thee that the light of the only Son of God has shone for those who dwell in darkness and in the shadow of death; it is by thee that the prophets announced the future, and that the apostles proclaim salvation to the nations, that the dead are raised, and that kings reign, in the name of the holy Trinity.

Is there any man who can worthily celebrate the praises of Mary? She is both mother and virgin. What a marvel! A marvel which overwhelms me! Who has ever heard it said that the builder would be prevented from dwelling in the temple that he himself had built? Could one dare to criticize the one who gives his servant the title of mother? The whole world rejoices . . . Let it be granted to us to venerate and adore the unity, to venerate and honour the indivisible Trinity, in singing the praises of Mary ever Virgin, that is to say of the holy church, and those of her son and immaculate spouse; for it is to him that glory belongs throughout all ages.

Homily pronounced at the Council of Ephesus (431)

---

that were oppressed by the devil, for God was with him' (Acts 10.38).

What we call the incarnation, then, is not just the event of the birth of Jesus or of his conception. For Jesus, to be man is much more than having a human nature, for which it would have

One of us

Who is Jesus? The first reply that occurs to one is simple: it is yours, it is mine; it is that of humanity for two thousand years; it consists of three words: one of us. There is an amazing certainty there. It delights the believer. It moves the unbeliever. Whoever we may be, in spite of our youth or our great age, our weakness, our ignorance or our poverty, we can tell ourselves: Jesus belongs to the same human race as I do. He has experienced my history. He has eaten the same daily bread. He was exposed to the same death. He is ours.

Daniel Pezeril, *Aujourd'hui Jesus*, Editions du Seuil, Paris 1973

been enough for him simply to have been born. It is to share in human destiny: a human birth, a human growth, a human education, a human trade, the joys and sufferings of a human being, the death of a human being. The incarnation is the long destiny of a human being, a destiny which had an origin but which does not have an end, in which all that is God has been incarnated for us.

A Christ who pretends?

The first disciples of Jesus, those who followed him, did not need people to tell them his history at length, still less to define his humanity. What could cause difficulties for them was the mystery of his identity, of his origin. 'Who is that . . .?' It took them time to arrive at the full revelation of the identity of Jesus as Son. But very soon the first generations, doubtless impressed by this revelation, were tempted to suspect or to neglect the human authenticity of Jesus. Dazzled by his glory, some of them came to imagine him half human, at any event not like us, and perhaps even pretending to be human (docetism). Besides, do not some Christians today have the confused feeling that Jesus only pretended to pray, or to be tempted, out of a concern to educate us, simply to show us how to do things?

Docetism: A Christ who pretends

God is immortal and impassible. How could the Son of God, God himself, suffer? To overcome the difficulty, some Christians produced the theory that he only seemed to suffer and die, or even that he only seemed to have a human body. This heresy is called docetism, from the Greek *dokein*, appear. At the time of the New Testament, St John reacted against this temptation by stressing the realism of the incarnation. We still find traces of this tendency in the way in which the Koran speaks of Jesus and his death.

There are not two Christs

The so-called Athanasian Creed was probably developed towards the end of the fifth century. It is common to the churches of both East and West; it is accepted by Protestants and Anglicans; for centuries it has been one of the most important points of reference for Western Christians This is what it says about Christ:

For the right faith is, that we believe and confess that our Lord Jesus Christ, the Son of God, is God and man.

God, of the substance of the Father, begotten before the worlds, and man, of the substance of his mother, born in the world. Perfect God and perfect man, of a reasonable soul and human flesh subsisting. Equal to the Father as touching his Godhead, and inferior to the Father as touching his manhood.

Who although he be God and man yet he is not two but one Christ; one not by conversion of the Godhead into flesh but by taking of the manhood into God. One altogether, not by confusion of substance but by unity of person. For as the reasonable soul and flesh is one man, so God and man is one Christ.

The Nativity. The Master of the Mills. Photo private collection

Do not divide Jesus Christ!

So it was necessary to clarify matters by explaining the humanity of Jesus, his human nature, which was no longer self-evident, in a definition of faith. At the Council of Chalcedon (451), 'Jesus truly God and truly man' became the expression of the faith of the Church. This is an affirmation that Jesus, the Christ, has two natures, his divine nature in which he is one with the Father, and his

---

The faith of Chalcedon

At the Council of Chalcedon, in 451, the Fathers, having solemnly reaffirmed the teaching of previous councils, in order to avoid controversies, added the following statements by way of further clarification:

Following, then, the holy Fathers, we all unanimously teach that our Lord Jesus Christ is to us one and the same Son, the self-same perfect in Godhead, the self-same perfect in manhood; truly God and truly man; the selfsame of a rational soul and body; consubstantial with the Father according to the Godhead, the selfsame consubstantial with us according to the manhood; like us in all things, sin apart; before the ages begotten of the Father as to the Godhead, but in the last days, the selfsame, for us and for our salvation of Mary the Virgin Theotokos as to the manhood; one and the same Christ, Son, Lord, only-begotten; acknowledged in two natures unconfusedly, unchangeably, indivisibly, inseparably; the difference of the natures being in no way removed because of the union, but rather the property of each nature being preserved, and both concurring into one prosopon and one hypostasis; not as though he were parted or divided into two prosopa, but one and the selfsame Son and only-begotten God, Word, Lord, Jesus Christ; even as from the beginning the prophets have taught concerning him, and as the Lord Jesus Christ himself has taught us, and as the symbol of the Fathers has handed down to us.

God in the human condition

He was born, in a miraculous fashion, from a woman according to the flesh. For it was impossible for him who was God by nature to become visible to the inhabitants of the earth in any other way than in a form similar to ours, invisible and incorporeal, without being made man and showing in himself and only in himself our nature bedecked with divine honours. For he was God in a form like ours. That is the sense in which we say that he became flesh and that is why we affirm that the Holy Virgin is Mother of God.

With the idea of incarnation is given all that is seen to arise out of this condition for the one who subjected himself to voluntary annihilation, for example hunger and weariness. In fact he was never weary, he who was almighty, nor could one talk of hunger in connection with the one who is the life and the food of all being, had he not appropriated a body made by nature for hunger and weariness. Similarly, one would never have counted him among the outcast – and that is why we say that he became sin – he would not have become a curse in suffering the cross for us, had he not become flesh, that is to say, had he not become incarnate and been made man by subjecting himself for us to a human birth like ours.

Cyril of Alexandria (died 444)

Jesus sleeping during
the tempest. Wood
engraving, fifteenth
century, Lyons.
Photo F. Garnier

The Multiplication of
the Loaves. Byzantine
Mosaic.
Photo F. Garnier

God made flesh that we might breathe the Spirit

'O thou who art beyond everything, how can I call thee by another name?' (Gregory of Nazianzus). The abyss beyond words, images, concepts, comes to us with the humanity of Christ. The whole history of the world is a gigantic movement of incarnation which is fulfilled in Christ, God made flesh, God made earth, assuming the maximum of humanity, freeing the prayer of the universe in such a way that bread is his body and wine his blood. He shows us definitively that we are not orphans, that the abyss of divinity constrains us like a mysterious paternal tenderness – Abba, Father – a maternal fatherhood, in the bowels of mercy in an almost uterine way, a liberating fatherhood which adopts us in his Son to communicate to us the breath which supports the worlds and sets our hearts aglow with a peace which is not of this world, in such a way that we can breathe the Spirit (Gregory the Sinaite), and become alive.

Olivier Clement, *Une brassée de confessions de foi*, Editions du Seuil, Paris 1979

---

human nature in which he is united with all of us. But this does not in any way affect the unity of his person, the unique person of the Son. Jesus God and man: this 'and' must not lead us to imagine a Christ cut in two, compartmentalized, having a kind of two-storey existence, on one of which he would be of us, exposed to the vicissitudes of human existence, and on the other of which he would be as it were turning in towards the Father. The two-fold solidarity of Christ is not dualism or duplicity; he is utterly committed to his human life, completely present in it and completely involved. Jesus is not a man part of the time (in his ministry and his suffering) and God the rest of the time (when he prays). Jesus is not man when he sleeps in the ship and God when he stills the tempest. Cyril of Alexandria, at the time of the Council of Ephesus, incessantly repeats: 'Do not divide Jesus Christ!' He does not let go of his divinity, that is to say his communion with the Father, for a moment: that is his identity. And his humanity, that is to say his solidarity with us, is never altered: it is the instrument, the expression of the divinity. Because God wanted to express himself in human existence (the Word was made flesh), a true human life became the word of God ('The flesh was made word', said St John Damescene).

Throughout his life

So the divinity of Jesus is not a state that he will have left to join us, an origin from which he will have been removed to bring himself close to us. The previous articles of the creed have made us see this as a relationship: the original and constitutive relationship between Jesus and his Father. Throughout his human life Jesus is Son, in a relationship which is his very being. And it is even that which is the absolute originality of the incarnation: a man has lived as Son of God; the Son of God has incarnated in a human life his relationship with the Father. Jesus, who is the Son from all eternity, because God has never been God without being Father, has never ceased to be the Son among us, even and above all in those moments of his human life which *a priori* might seem to us to be the most remote from the idea that we might have of God: for example in the apparent insignificance of his childhood, in his weakness, his weariness, his sleep, his moments of discouragement or anger, but above all, of course, in his sufferings and in his death.

For Jesus, then, to be God is not to bear on his shoulders a supplementary nature which would blot out his humanity. It is to experience with God a communion of such a kind that it manifests the unique and original bond which he has with God. Jesus is aware of this bond, and all the evangelists bear witness to it. No one has had to reveal it to him or to teach it to him. His first recorded words speak of the Father (Luke 2.49). But this awareness of a proximity, of a communion, of an immediacy with the Father has not to be imagined as including a universal knowledge of beings and events. Jesus does not stand outside history. He does not pull its threads like a puppet master. Events surprise him. We must not project on to his human consciousness all that we imagine of God. Jesus can explain his relationship with God only with words drawn from our human experience: being father, being son, not knowing the last hour (Mark 13.32) is not incompatible, for Jesus, with the certainty that everything is in the hands of the Father and that he is himself everything to him.

Truly man because truly God

How in fact does it come about that the humanity and divinity of Jesus are so often seen as opposites? People often use terms indicating concession, as if Jesus was God though man, or man though God. It is as if there was always a risk of going too far in affirming one of his natures and by the same token of forgetting the other. A balance ought to be kept. Are we not the prisoners of ideas that we have of humanity and God?

'No one has seen God at any time: the only Son who is in the bosom of the Father, has revealed him to us' (John 1.18). It is the same on the human side. And if it is true that human beings are above all characterized by openness to others, by a capacity for relationship, a vocation to communion; if it is true that the God whom Jesus unveils to us is himself self-giving, sharing, ecstasy towards the other, trinitarian communion, it is no longer possible to affirm that to be God and to be man are necessarily incompatible. It is not a matter of confusing human nature and divine nature but of remembering that human beings were created in the image of God, precisely in order one day to allow a man to be the perfect image, the definitive icon. With Nicaea, it is important to distinguish the Son, who is begotten of the Father, and our condition of being created; but while at the same time seeing that all creation finds its fulfilment by being taken up again into the incarnation of the one who remains the only one begotten of the Father. Human beings are not God, but human beings are made for God. In Jesus we discover that this is his nature, his vocation. Human beings are not nothing: they are capable of God.

So one can say that Jesus is truly man, not although he is God, but precisely because he is truly God. It is because God is God, faithful to his word, entirely committed in his action towards us, that Jesus did not trifle with our humanity and the conditions in which we live. God does not engage in make-believe. And it is because Jesus is true Son of God that he could bring to perfection human nature and human vocation, which is a matter of opening oneself, in an act of thanksgiving, to the Fatherhood of the one who is the source of our life. To be Son is finally the supreme way of being man: for Jesus first of all, then for us, in and by his Spirit.

15   Crucified, Dead and Buried

By taking as their emblem the cross of Jesus, Christians issued a challenge: so they were mocked as initiates of a crucified Messiah – all right, they would be proud of that cross (see I Cor. 1)!

The death, or more precisely the execution, of Jesus, is at the centre of the creed. It is even the first event mentioned after Jesus' birth. The Apostles' Creed proclaims that Jesus was born of the Virgin Mary, suffered under Pontius Pilate, was crucified, dead and buried. And the Nicene Creed: He was made man. Crucified for us under Pontius Pilate he suffered his passion and was buried. Suffering, crucifixion, death, burial: with such stress that it seems as though the main event of the life of Jesus was his death.

Dr Couchoud and the historicity of Jesus

According to the testimony of Jean Guitton, Paul-Louis Couchoud was ready to accept the whole creed apart from the expression 'Under Pontius Pilate . . .':

I have recently come to know M. Paul-Louis Couchoud, philosopher, doctor, exegete, analyst, acute observer of everything, whose works I have read with curiosity, being amazed by this unprecedented paradox which he has put forward: Jesus is the greatest person to have existed in history, and even today is the greatest inhabitant of the earth, but he did not exist in the historical sense of the word: he was not born, he did not suffer under Pontius Pilate. All that is a mystical fabulation.

Having lost his faith, which is not in our power, he said, quoting Pascal, and which alone would have allowed him to take the texts of the Gospels in their full sense, without subjecting them to a perilous process of selection, being unable to make use of the scissors of the scholar Loisy, who ended up by reducing Jesus to being no more than a poor man who hardly existed – he would have preferred to admit that this minimum of existence should be annulled in turn and argue that Jesus-God-and-man existed only for faith. In saying this he was not thinking of diminishing faith in Jesus. In his eyes, Jesus had first of all been thought of as God. God had died for us, the lamb who was sacrificed. He was like an atemporal living being sacrificed mystically in a kind of eternal mass. But to satisfy those who were smitten with history, that inferior genre of knowledge, Jesus-God was garbed in an anecdotal humanity, an utterly improbable biography. I would guess that this view represented a quest for security. In concluding that Jesus did not exist in history, Dr Couchoud thought he was giving him a super-existence which was invulnerable to doubt.

Jean Guitton, *Jesus*, Gramet, Paris 1956

Under Pontius Pilate

Apart from Jesus and Mary, one human being has honour done to him in the creed, Pontius Pilate. Doubtless he did not think that he would become a celebrity as a result of this skimpy trial, and yet he has an important role for us: he anchors the history of Jesus in the mainstream of the history of his time. By confronting Jesus with the power of Rome, he definitively roots Jesus in the history written by historians, to such a degree that those who would want to make Jesus an atemporal myth, a revelation of human destiny without historical reality, are offended by this sentinel who continues to watch by the cross. That is doubtless why the creed holds on to Pontius Pilate.

A historian who did not share in the Christian faith could, however, say something about Jesus. He could give his own opinion on the testimony of the Gospels and these first Christian communities, but also take into account the several traces of the emergences of Christianity in the non-Christian literature of the time. He could also compare this evidence with what one can reconstitute of contemporary Jewish traditions and with archaeological discoveries about Palestine in the time of Jesus. So there are some points about Jesus on which the majority of historians are agreed: his original link with Baptist circles, the originality of his behaviour and above all his execution, with a trial combining a religious cause and political implications, the cross, a Roman punishment.

Jesus in pagan literature

Outside the New Testament, we have few mentions of Jesus in the literature of his time. But these few allusions are infinitely more than we have to the majority of his contemporaries.

– A letter from the procounsul Pliny to the emperor Trajan (no. 96, written in 110). This is a report on the activity of Christians in his province. Pliny describes how they meet on a particular day, before dawn, to sing a hymn to Christ as to a god, and how they pledge themselves to behave honourably.

– In the *Annals* of Tacitus (XV.44, a text written about 115), the Roman historian speaks of Christians persecuted by Nero and says specifically: 'Their name comes from Christ, who was executed in the reign of Tiberius by the procurator Pontius Pilate, and this detestable superstition, quenched for a while, revived and has

spread not only through Judaea, where all the abominations of the earth find their place and their devotees.'

– In his *Life of Claudius* (emperor from 14 to 54), Suetonius reports (around 120) that the emperor expelled the Jews from Rome because under the influence of Chrestus they were causing considerable unrest.

– Two letters of the emperor Hadrian (117–137) mention Christians. One gives instructions for trying them in Asia Minor. The other speaks ironically of bishops of Christ in Egypt who can both venerate Serapis and prostrate themselves before Christ.

– Lucian, a satirical author writing in Greek about 170, mocks Christians and their 'crucified sophist'.

A scandal

Why this death? Before even looking at its meaning we ought to determine its causes more precisely. The Christian tradition has developed answers, and catechesis has forged phrases: Jesus died for our sins, his sacrifice gives life. However, these phrases sometimes risk making us forget the shock that the failure and execution of their master gave to the first disciples.

Besides, it is not to easy to reconstruct the chain of events and the exact responsibility of each of those involved. The sentence and execution were Roman. But the political charge ('He stirs up the people', Luke 23.5; 'Everyone who makes himself a king sets himself against Caesar', John 19.12) seems rather to be the legal dressing of another trial: 'They asked Pilate for his death', ran the very first catechesis handed down in the Acts of the Apostles (13.28). The real conflict was religious, and beyond the accusations about the sabbath or about the Temple, it related to God himself. This question must have been vital for Jesus and fatal for the religious authorities for such a break to come about. It is also possible the political and religious imbroglio even received the endorsement of the people when the governor asked the crowd: 'What then shall I do with Jesus who is called Messiah?' and all replied, 'Let him be crucified!' (Matt. 27.22). So a whole society united against him.

Did the disciples deserve the reproaches of Jesus ('O foolish men, and slow of heart to believe all that the prophets have spoken!', Luke 24.25) for having failed to discern in the scriptures the announcement of such a dismal end for the Messiah? Jesus raised could suggest a different interpretation to them: *a posteriori*, and in the light of Easter, certain texts explained themselves (Luke 24.26–27, 45–46). But it must be recognized that for the believing Jews of the time, and today, they do not leap to the eyes. Hence the disappointment of the first disciples in the logic of Peter's violent reaction at the time of the first announcement of the Passion (Matt. 16.22) 'But we had hoped that he was the one to redeem Israel' (Luke 24.21).

Jesus seen by a Jew of his time

Flavius Josephus, born in Jerusalem around 37, who died at the end of the first century, wrote several works on the history of his people. In one of them, the *Jewish Antiquities*, there are a number of mentions of Jesus. These texts have been disputed. It is not impossible that they have been retouched by Christians, but many critics see them as evidence of prime importance about Jesus. This is the most distinctive passage:

Towards this time Jesus arose, a wise man, if he must truly be called man. For he did miraculous things and taught people who received the truth with pleasure, and he won over to his cause numerous Jews and also numerous Greeks. He was the Christ. And when on the accusation of the most important men among us Pilate had him condemned to the cross, those who had loved him first did not cease to know him; for he appeared to them the third day alive again, since the divine prophets had predicted this and ten thousand other miraculous things about him. And even now the tribe of Christians named after him is not extinct.

The triumph of hatred

In the first catechesis, after the resurrection, the execution of Jesus is far from being presented as salvation. Quite the opposite: the inhabitants of Jerusalem and their leaders had killed Jesus but God had intervened to snatch him from death and that was salvation (see Acts 2.23–24; 13.27–30). In the parable of the murderers in the vineyard, the assassination of the Son, a paroxysm in the escalation of violence unleashed against the prophets, is not a gesture of salvation but the height of sin. And it is the intervention of the owner which remedies the situation: 'The very stone which the builders rejected has become the head of the corner; this was the Lord's doing and it is marvellous in our eyes!' (Mark 12.10–11). In that way the resurrection is prefigured.

For Christians, the execution of Jesus remains a scandal, a stumbling block to the enthusiasm of those who follow him. 'For Jews demand signs and Greeks seek wisdom, but we preach Christ crucified, a stumbling-block to Jews and folly to Gentiles . . .' (I Cor. 1.22–23). It is important for this scandal not be minimized, for believers not to get used in some way to the death of Jesus. Despite everything, at a superficial level this death to which Jesus gave meaning remains a setback to his mission, and the tangible sign that in our history hatred has at least the word before last.

Jesus transforms his death

If the power and wisdom of God could be shown in this setback and in this punishment of the cross (I Cor. 1.23), it is not thanks to those who wanted the trial and execution. That is why Jesus himself returned, to transform his death. 'For the foolishness of God is wiser than men, and the weakness of God is stronger than men' (1.25). The cross is not the exaltation of suffering, of weakness, and of those who exploit it to dominate the world. It is the exaltation of the one who could transform suffering and weakness into a capacity to love.

So it is not the death of Christ which saves us, otherwise his executioners would be our saviours. It is love which he lives out to the death. His death takes on the meaning that he wants to give it, the meaning that he had already given to the whole of his life: like all his life, all his actions, it becomes language, word, sign, a testimony to what makes him alive. Here, at the highest point, the flesh becomes word.

The death of Jesus seems in effect to be an encounter, a clash, between two logics: the logic of Jesus, who wants to express to us the universal love of the Father at the risk of provoking the violent reaction of those to whom that poses a threat, and the logic of rejection, the logic of those who are ready to do anything to keep him quiet.

Just as the light accuses the shade, so the death of Jesus denounces sin: it comes to light in the unleashing of this hatred, this power of death ('The devil was a murderer from the beginning', John 8.44). It has to be seen. And at the same moment the death of Jesus is a testimony to grace: it shows us that Jesus did not love by halves. He did not capitulate to the threat. He did not renounce his mission or tone it down. 'Having loved his own who were in the world, he loved them to the end' (John 13.1).

No one takes my life

So the death of Jesus is not an accident. Granted, he did not look for it, as if with a kind of death wish. He did not provoke it, as if it had itself been the will of the Father. The will of the Father is not the death of the Son but his mission of loving to the end and to express the boundlessness of the love of God, even in this death. That is why Jesus did not shun it.

By his death he left a mark on his life. The cross is like a seal which authenticates all that he has

84

Jesus presented to the people. Engraving. Detail. Rijksmuseum, Amsterdam. Photo private collection

done so far. It was *necessary*, not as a blind destiny or as a vocation to death, but as the logic of his own life, and as the logic of the whole history of salvation as that history had already been manifested in the scriptures: God does not love by halves.

Jesus underwent his death. But one can also say that he chose it. He did not choose the events which took place, the opponents who were in league against him, Herod and Pilate who were reconciled over him. But on these events which were out of his hands he chose to inscribe and explain that for which he came, that by which and for which he is. 'No one takes my life from me, but I lay it down of my own accord' (John 10.18), he can say when people are trying to lay hands on him. His life is not out of his hands nor is his death. He has taken his life into his hands to offer it to the Father in a gesture of blessing and thanksgiving. He has taken into his hands his life, all the moments of which were given, to hold it out to us like a piece of bread to be shared. 'Take eat, this is me, this is my body.' It is a life which was already wholly given, shared, eaten.

Why the death of the Son?

So we can see why the death of the Son can be a source of salvation through the love that it expresses. Why the death? In each moment of his life Jesus inscribed, translated, incarnated the love of the Father for us. Tradition repeated this: the least of his actions, full of an infinite love, would have been enough to save us. But only in death does a person thus put himself completely

---

When a Christian wants to live out the passion

Ignatius, Bishop of Antioch around 110, writes to the Christians of Rome not to intervene on his behalf in order to enable him to escape martyrdom:

The ends of the earth and the kingdoms of the world shall profit me nothing. It is better for me to die in Christ Jesus than to be king over the ends of the earth. I seek him who died for our sake. I desire him who rose for us. The pains of birth are upon me. Suffer me, my brethren; hinder me not from living, do not wish me to die. Do not give to the world one who desires to belong to God, nor deceive him with material things. Suffer me to receive the pure light; when I have come thither I shall become a man. Suffer me to follow the example of the passion of my God. If any man have him within himself, let him understand what I wish, and let him sympathize with me, knowing the things which constrain me.

The prince of this world wishes to tear me in pieces, and to corrupt my mind towards God. Let none of you who are present help him. Be rather on my side, that is on God's. Do not speak of Jesus Christ, and yet desire the world. Let no envy dwell among you. Even though when I come I beseech you myself, do not be persuaded by me, but rather obey this, which I write to you; for in the midst of life I write to you desiring death. My lust has been crucified, and there is in me no fire of love for material things; but only water living and speaking in me, and saying to me from within, 'Come to the Father.' I have no pleasure in the food of corruption or in the delights of this life. I desire the bread of God, which is the flesh of Jesus Christ, who was of the seed of David, and for drink I desire his blood, which is incorruptible love.

Ignatius of Antioch, *Letter to the Romans*, 6.1–7.3

in the hands of the one who accepts him. Only in death does he dispossess himself of everything in order to receive himself from the one who alone gave him birth. If Jesus experienced his death in this way, it is not *although* he was the Son but *because* he is the Son. The universal vocation of humankind, to put oneself in the hands of the Father, could thus be lived out to the end only by the one who is the Son, one with the Father from all eternity. If the death of the Son of God can seem logical to us here, with the revolutionary logic of the divine purposes, that is not because of its worth, which would be the only compensation for the offence, as if God found satisfaction in it. It is by reason of Jesus' filial capacity for communion. Only the Son whose whole life was communion with the Father, since it is his very being to be in the bosom of the Father (John 1.18), could have a death in such a communion.

Head of Christ. Sculpture. Photo F. Garnier

Jesus will be in agony until the end of the world

I believe that Jesus only complained this one time, but then he complained as if he could not contain his excessive sadness: 'My soul is sorrowful even unto death.'

Jesus sought company and relief from men and women. It seems to me that that is a unique feature of his life. But he did not receive any then, for his disciples slept.

Jesus will be in agony until the end of the world; we must not sleep during this time . . .

Console yourself; you would not seek me if you had not found me. I thought of you in my agony, I shed such drops of blood for you.

Blaise Pascal, *The Mystery of Jesus*

God-given

God is not the instigator of this death. He does not stand before his dying Son as though he laid claim to him in some way. He is as always with him and in him. He is implicated, handed over, murdered on his side: God-given.

'The Son can do nothing of himself, but only that which he sees the Father do' (John 5.19). This is true of all the actions of Jesus, of all his words: the Father must always be seen at work in them, and *a fortiori* in his last work. In Jesus who loves to the end, it is God who unveils himself, who expresses himself, who hands himself over. So we are a long way from theories which would want to see the death of Jesus as a demand of his Father, at the risk of making us imagine an executioner god. Contemporary atheism could well have found there one of its sources or its justifications.

Having followed Jesus throughout his career, the disciple who arrives at the foot of the cross is then called to raise his or her eyes towards the crucified one to recognize there the final and disconcerting revelation of God which Jesus has always given. It is there that the strongest expressions in Christian faith about the unity of the Father and the Son take on meaning. It is in the perspective of the cross that one must understand sayings of Jesus like: 'He who has seen me has seen the Father' (John 14.9); 'I and the Father are one (John 10.30). And it is there that the disciple can say in response, 'He is the image of the invisible God' (Col. 1.15).

On the cross Jesus, with perfect love, loving to the end, perfectly resembles the one who sends him: he is his icon, the Word. The Word was made flesh, that is to say fragile, vulnerable; but also tangible, manifested, given. And it is then that we see his glory (John 1.14), his communion with the Father, the glory which he takes from his father as the only Son. This glory does not wait for the resurrection in order to manifest itself; it is the filial radiance shown in every work of Jesus, his complete resemblance to the Father, the aura of his divinity over the least of his actions. For the disciple whom Jesus loves and whom he allows to follow him so far, it bursts out on the cross. 'When you have lifted up the Son of man, then you will know that I am' (John 8.28).

Far from contradicting or veiling the divinity of Jesus, as a provisional concession to the weakness of our humanity, the cross expresses God, a capacity for loving and a power of life. The cross unveils God.

16   Risen and Exalted

'If Christ has not been raised, your faith is futile and you are still in your sins. Then those also who have fallen asleep in Christ have perished. If in this life we who are in Christ have only hope, we are of all men most to be pitied' (I Cor. 15.17–19). Other believers hope for the resurrection of the dead at the end of time, but faith in the resurrection of Jesus that has already taken place, and that inaugurates a new life for us today, is the most radical and new feature of our creed. The resurrection is even the source of the whole creed: it is in the light of Easter that Jesus appears fully Son of God: there we are given the Spirit which is the foundation of the church: there the God of life is manifested in the fruitfulness of his Fatherhood.

God raised him

In the New Testament the work of the resurrection of Jesus is primarily attributed to his Father: God has raised him. This is particularly the case in the great evangelization discourses reported by the Acts of the Apostles (see Acts 2.24,36; 3.12; 4.10; 5.31; 10.40; 13.30,33,34,37). Here the God of life takes the opposite view to our words of death: You crucified him; God raised him. God overturns the judgment, restores justice. He raises up the one who has been abased.

At the same time he responds to the love of the one who has loved him so far. If the death of Jesus is the utterly filial action of the one who puts himself entirely in the hands of God, the resurrection is the fatherly response of the one who accepts this gift and who welcomes his Son into his communion of life. In his death Jesus is

shown to be fully Son. In his resurrection, God is shown to be fully Father: 'He raised Jesus, as it is written in the second Psalm: You are my Son, today I have begotten you' (Acts 13.33, quoting Ps. 2.7).

And Jesus is so much one with the Father who gives and restores life that he is associated with this work of his own resurrection, as with all the works of the Father. He receives his resurrection, but he does not undergo it. He participates in its very source. 'As the Father has life in himself, so he has granted the Son also to have life in himself' (John 5.26). 'In him was life' (John 1.4). That is why he can say, 'I have power to lay down my life and I have power to take it up again' (John 10.18). The Christian tradition will retain this participation of the Son in his own resurrection by saying that he raised himself. That does not detract in any way from the work of the Father: it manifests it. In the same trinitarian logic the Spirit is present and active in the resurrection of Jesus, as in every work of God, from the first creation to our last re-creation. 'If the Spirit of him who raised Jesus from the dead dwells in you, he who raised Christ Jesus from the dead will give life to your mortal bodies also through his Spirit which dwells in you' (Rom. 8.11).

He showed himself

The affirmation of the resurrection is based on the witness of those who, after the death of Jesus, met him alive. No one claims to have seen him coming forth from the tomb. But men and women had a quite unique encounter in which

Jesus, the crucified one, showed himself, taking the initiative to make himself known. Several lists of witnesses circulated in the communities. St Paul, from shortly after his conversion and the questions put to him by the risen Christ, has given us one of the most extended and apparently the earliest (see I Cor. 15.3). Each evangelist, for the needs of his catechesis, has more specifically recorded one or other of these encounters, all of which end with a collegiate encounter with the eleven, the basis of their mission.

If the resurrection was primarily a spectacular proof of the deity of Jesus and the mission he received from the Father, it would have been appropriate by our logic for the Risen Christ also, indeed primarily, to have shown himself to his adversaries and all those who had rejected him. Now the encounter with the risen Christ remains the experience of the circle of disciples: 'God raised him on the third day and made him manifest; not to all the people but to us who were chosen by God as witnesses who ate and drank with him after he rose from the dead' (Acts

---

The triumph of the Risen Christ

He arose from the dead
to the heights of the heavens,
God who put on man,
and suffered for the sufferer,
and was bound for him who was bound,
and judged for him who was condemned,
and buried for him who was buried.

And he arose from the dead and cries thus:
'Who is he that contends against me?
Let him stand before me.
I freed the condemned,
I made the dead to live again,
I raised him who was buried.
Who is he who raises his voice against me?
I,' he says, 'am the Christ,
I am he who put down death,
and triumphed over the enemy,
and trod upon Hades,
and bound the strong one
and brought man safely home
to the heights of heaven;
I,' he says, 'Christ.'

Therefore come all you families of men,
who are sullied with sins,
and receive remission of sins.

For I am your remission.
I am the Passover of salvation,
the Lamb that was sacrificed for you,
I am your ransom,
I am your light,
I am your saviour,
I am the resurrection,
I am your king,
I lead you up to the heights of the heavens,
I will show you the Father
who is from the ages,
I will raise you up by my right hand.

This is he who first made heaven and earth,
who in the beginning created man,
who was proclaimed by Law and Prophets,
who was made flesh in a virgin,
who was hanged on a tree,
who was buried in the earth,
who rose from the dead
and went up to the heights of heaven.

The earliest Easter homily that has come down to us (second century).

Text from *The Homily on the Passion by Melito, Bishop of Sardis*, ed. Campbell Bonner, University of Pennsylvania Press 1940, p.180

The Resurrection.
Detail. El Greco,
Prado Museum,
Madrid.
Photo Giraudon

10.40–41).

Apart from St Paul, who does not seem to have known Jesus according to the flesh, the witnesses to the risen Christ had been prepared for this encounter by all the catechesis from before Easter. For them recognition of the risen Jesus was primarily a reunion. That did not prevent some of them from beginning by hesitating or doubting. The Easter faith, the luminous discovery of the living Jesus, does not present itself as the fruit of their regrets or their nostalgia, but as the resurrection of their faith from before Easter, which had died with the death of Jesus, and was again evoked by an encounter in which he himself took the initiative.

However, the focus of this encounter is not the evocation of old memories. 'Do not hold me!' says Jesus to Mary Magdalene when she clings to the former memories of her master (John 20.17). The risen Christ directs us towards the future and towards mission: 'Go and say to his disciples and to Peter . . .' (Mark 16.7); 'Go and find my brothers and tell them . . .' (John 20.17), 'Go, make disciples of all nations . . .' (Matt. 28.19).

The third day

The expression already occurs in the very ancient short creed of which Paul reminds the Corinthians: 'He rose again on the third day according to the scriptures' (I Cor. 15.4). We also find it in two different forms in the announcements by Jesus of his passion: 'It was necessary . . . that he should be put to death and that three days later he should rise again' (Mark 8.31; 10.34). 'He must be put to death and the third day rise again' (Matt. 16.21). Mark's formula, which seems earlier, could denote the third day after the one mentioned. Matthew would have transposed it into the manner of speaking of his time.

In the Gospel accounts of Easter, this notion reappears to locate in time the encounters with the Risen Christ; on the Emmaus Road the disciples, recalling the crucifixion, say in order to explain their despair: 'And more than that, this is the third day since all this happened' (Luke 24.21). All the narratives fix the event of the resurrection of Jesus on the first day of the week, the day after the sabbath (Matt. 28.1; Mark 16.2; Luke 24.1; John 20.1). The third day after the death of Jesus thus becomes the Lord's Day ('At dawn on the Lord's Day . . .' writes the Gospel of Peter, an apocryphal text), and began to be celebrated as such (Acts 20.7; Rev. 1.10), from Sunday to Sunday (cf. John 20.19,26).

But behind this chronological indication and this liturgical tradition the expression 'the third day' has a theological significance which is even more important. In the biblical tradition it served to evoke the last days, the time when God will finally console, save and raise his people. Eight centuries before Jesus, the prophet Hosea already expressed this hope: 'God has stricken, and he will bind up our wounds. After two days he will revive us; on the third day he will raise us up that we may live before him' (6.1–2).

The disciples of Jesus were aware that in his resurrection this final salvation had been inaugurated. That meant that it was not just some figures of the Old Testament who took on significance (like Jonah, who remained three days in the belly of the sea monster, cf. Matt. 12.40); all scriptures promising salvation had been fulfilled. 'He was raised the third day according to the scriptures.' And the Fourth Gospel, already contemplating the glory of the Risen Christ in each of Jesus' actions and signs, could begin the story of the first of them like this: 'The third day there was a wedding at Cana in Galilee' (John 2.1; cf. also Luke 2.46).

He descended into hell

The Apostles' Creed mentions this descent to hell between the burial and the resurrection of Jesus. What is this descent, and what is the hell?

It is not hell as we understand it today, a situation of perdition which is the prison for those who radically and definitively turn away from God, an eternal punishment to which they condemn themselves, in the painful absence of the source of life. But the hell in which the Christ makes himself present is the place where the dead are, what Judaism calls Sheol; in the symbolic representation of the time it is the lower place (in Latin *infernum*), very remote from God Most High.

Contrary to what certain theologians thought at the Reformation, then, Jesus did not take on himself the pains of hell in our place, as a punishment which the Father brought on the Son (the same theologians interpreted the prayer of Christ on the cross in the same way as an abandonment, a punishment by the Father). It is hard to see how that would save us, but we can see very clearly the non-Christian God whom it would reveal.

So in the logic of the incarnation, the descent into hell is the will of God, in his Christ, to reestablish and revive human life. It is the ultimate fulfilment of this desire for presence and communion, of this project of salvation and resurrection. St Peter attests it: the good news has been announced even to the dead; Jesus went to preach even to the spirits in prison (I Peter 4.6;. 3.19). The Greek Fathers, Origen, Gregory of Nazianzus, Cyril of Alexandria, John Damascene and John Chrysostom all interpret the descent into hell as a mystery of salvation. It is the power

of the Risen Christ, his liberating Word, which thus reaches out not only to the contemporaries of Jesus of Nazareth and those who find themselves on the path of his disciples, but to people of all centuries, of all generations. Thus everyone is mysteriously visited by Christ, even in his or her death.

In the East, the icon of the descent into hell is a favourite representation of the resurrection: Christ in white clothes, already in the glory of the resurrection, comes to the place of the dead, passing through the gates of hell, which have been thrown down and lie in the form of a cross. He stretches out his hand to Adam, the fallen man, behind whom throng a crowd of kings, prophets, and anonymous figures, all those who in advance of him set their hope on him, those who lived for him without yet seeing him. He appeared to those who were in darkness and in the shadow of death (Luke 1.79). Finally, they could encounter him.

In the light of this mystery of the descent into hell, missionaries, announcing the gospel of Christ to peoples who are very preoccupied with the cult of the dead and the salvation of their ancestors, have been able to bear witness that the reviving power of the risen Christ thus reaches all men and women, those who prepared for his coming from afar. 'When he ascended on high he left a host of captives . . . In saying "He ascended", what does it mean but that he had also descended into the lower parts of the earth? He who descended is also he who ascended far above all the heavens, that he might fill all things' (Eph. 4.5–10). From now on no one, even though dead, no creature, is alien to Jesus Christ.

The open tomb

The tomb of Jesus was found open and empty. In itself this emptiness does not express the depth of the resurrection, Jesus in the glory of the Father. But at the time when the Gospels were being written the adversaries of Jesus were putting round another interpretation: the disciples had come to snatch away the body of their master (see Matt. 28.11–15). This was a sign that at least they did not dispute that the tomb had been found empty.

It is the encounter with the living Jesus which gives full meaning to the openness of this tomb. Intrinsically the sign of an absence, the empty tomb then becomes the announcement of a presence. In the birth of faith in the resurrection, the first role of the tomb of Jesus seems to have been to connect the announcement of the resurrection with the last episodes of the passion: the same place, the same witnesses, the group of holy women. It is aimed at attesting the continuity, the rejoining of the thread of life: the risen Christ is the crucified Jesus.

If the Christian communities so cherished the remembrance of a first journey by the women to the tomb in the first light of the first day of the week, it is doubtless because they saw this as the model for many journeys, pilgrimages: the disciples continued to converge on the place of the death of Jesus, to be told solemnly, by a spokesman of the God of life, that they should no longer seek Christ in the pious memories of the past where the dead are embalmed; from then on he would always await them elsewhere, among their brothers and sisters, among the mixed nations of Galilee, in the fresh air of mission.

The tomb of Jesus, void of his body and filled with the announcement of his resurrection, is an important element of Easter faith. Even if among present-day Christians, stamped by centuries of Hellenism, some people may suppose that the essential thing is the way in which Jesus is present to us, rather than the disappearance of the material molecules which made up his body, it is clear that for the disciples, in their semitic realism, it was unthinkable to believe in Jesus alive while knowing that his body was decomposing.

The body of the Risen Christ

Jesus is not Lazarus. His resurrection, only prefigured in all the actions in which he was shown to be the master of life, is not a simple reanimation. Having emerged from the tomb, Lazarus returned, for a limited reprieve of earthly life. Definitively snatched from death, Jesus entered into God's future. And those who saw him alive again had a unique experience, going beyond simple observation by their senses: challenged in their faith, and even tempted to doubt, they saw something of his glory, that is to say his original proximity to the Father, from henceforth casting its rays on all his humanity. A body of flesh sown in the earth, the risen Christ is a spiritual body (I Cor. 15.44); not a dematerialized body but completely invested with the Holy Spirit. Jesus risen is a new creation.

This new creation took hold of Jesus in all that he was, in all that he is, body and soul. In him the whole person is transfigured and saved. His resurrection is not a kind of immaterial apotheosis.

All through the life of Jesus of Nazareth his body was his presence in the world, his actions, his words, his look, his way of being there. That is not something that Jesus could have possessed provisionally and which he would have used as an instrument, subsequently to abandon it. It is Jesus himself as he externalizes himself. Hence this expression of himself which brings about the prodigious realism of the incarnation cannot be excluded by his glorification.

Thus the resurrection which is expected for the end of time was inaugurated in a unique way in

Jesus of Nazareth. To say that this body was taken up into glory is to say that the new creation takes form in the old. It is to look at this material, corporeal world with all that can rise up in it to make it more loving, more communicative, the very material from which the kingdom of God will be made.

Christ in limbo.
Fresco. Detail. Kahriye Djami, Istanbul.
Photo Boudot-Lamotte

17 He Will Come Again in Glory

Every time that Christians remember Jesus in their eucharist, they sing: 'We proclaim your death, Lord Jesus, we celebrate your resurrection, we await your coming in glory.'

He will come again

Thus at the very moment when they recognize and adore the real presence of the Lord, they comfort one another with the hope: He will come again! So has he gone? Is he absent?

The Ascension marked the end of a certain mode of presence for which the first Christian communities were still nostalgic: 'Men of Galilee, why do you stand looking into heaven? This Jesus, who was taken up from you into heaven, will come in the same way as you saw him go into heaven' (Acts 1.11). This departure is not, however, an absence. Jesus promised that he would remain with his followers until the end of time (Matt. 28.20). And from now on he envelops them in the discreet omnipresence of his Spirit.

But in its prayer the church desires all the more ardently the return of its Lord and Master: 'The Spirit and the Bride say, "Come." Amen, come Lord Jesus' (Rev. 22.17,20).

Every year the liturgy makes us relive the expectation of this coming, Latin *adventus*, in the season of Advent. Not to pretend that we are in the time before the nativity, as contemporaries of Abraham, Isaac or John the Baptist, but to stir up in us a desire for this manifest return. This is no longer the expectation of the birth of Jesus, the germinal presence, barely noticeable, of the Lord of glory in a corner of our planet, in a fugitive instant of our history, but the expectation of the day when he will be all in all, he who is already something in the heart of everyone. And in this new expectation, for us Christians the Israel of today, which still keeps watch for the Messiah, remains the prophet of hope.

The time of Advent, of coming, thus reminds the church, tempted as it is, to drowse over its memories, of the existence of millions of men and women for whom Christ has not yet come. There were those who lived before him in history, some of whom could prepare for his day: 'These all died in faith, not having received what was promised, but having seen it and greeted it from afar . . .' (Heb. 11.13); 'Abraham your father rejoiced to see my day: he saw it and was transported with joy' (see also the box on page 93 on the descent into hell). And there are also all those who today still live before Christ and towards him, because they have not encountered his gospel.

A time of hope, Advent is thus the time of mission, the time when the Spirit mobilizes the church so that Christ can continue to take form in human history, in the diversity of our civilizations, our cultures, our mentalities, our most human hopes. The logic of the incarnation thus continues in what is called in our modern jargon the indigenization of faith, the inculturation of the gospel, that is to say the irruption of Christ into new human realities to convert them and lead them to their fulfilment.

To the degree that the Christ has not been welcomed, understood, translated, sung, experienced, in all mentalities, cultures and spiritual quests which have marked humanity and will mark it to the end of time, something of

Christ in Glory. Tympanum of Vézelay Cathedral. Photo private collection

the fullness of Christ will be absent. And the church, which must become his body, will continue in expectation, in hope. As an invitation to watch in prayer and, in direct connection with that, to mobilize in mission: 'We await, we prepare your coming in glory.'

Should we still expect him?

Expectation – anxious, collective and operative expectation of an end of the world, that is to say of an issue for the world – that is perhaps the supreme Christian function and the most distinctive characteristic of our religion.

Historically speaking, that expectation has never ceased to guide the progress of our faith like a torch. The Israelites were constantly expectant, and the first Christians too. Christmas, which might have been thought to turn our gaze towards the past, has only fixed it further in the future. The Messiah, who appeared for a moment in our midst, only allowed himself to be seen and touched for a moment before vanishing once again, more luminous and ineffable than ever, into the depths of the future. He came. Yet now we must expect him – no longer a small chosen group among us, but all men – once again and more than ever. The Lord Jesus will only come soon if we ardently expect him. It is an accumulation of desires that should cause the Pleroma to burst upon us.

Successors to Israel, we Christians have been charged with keeping the flame of desire ever alive in the world. Only twenty centuries have passed since the Ascension. What have we made of our expectancy?

Pierre Teilhard de Chardin, *Le Milieu Divin*, Epilogue, 'In Expectation of the Parousia', Collins 1960; Fount 1969, p. 151

The judgment of the world

How can we await this coming with such impatience if we are to be judged in it? Do we have to await in terror the Christ who comes to judge the living and the dead? Is the Last Judgment of Michaelangelo in the Sistine Chapel, in which the Christ raises his arms above the multitudes of terror-stricken bodies, really Christian?

The judgment to come must without doubt be understood in the logic of the first coming of Christ. The Christ who says, 'It is for judgment that I am come' (John 9.31), explains to Nicodemus: 'For God sent the Son into the world, not to condemn the world, but that the world might be saved through him' (John 3.17). Judgment is crucial at this instant, this moment of truth, in which each person must determine himself or herself. In the presence of Christ who is light, life and truth, each individual is called on to choose: there are those who choose light, and those who shut themselves up in death and choose darkness, because their works are evil (3.19). Judgment is the incompatibility of light with darkness, of life with death. It illuminates, it denounces, it accuses, making us arise from this kind of intermediate stage in which we enjoy ourselves.

Nowadays, when someone discovers the gospel of Christ, when a catechumen asks for baptism, this judgment is already at work. The incompatibility of the gospel with all the aspects of his or her personal, family or professional life appears. He or she is aware that the word of God cuts like a sword through life, demanding painful sacrifices, upsetting priorities. The light of Christ accuses his or her darkness. And after baptism, this person will have this experience again all his or her life, in every examination of conscience, in every penitential liturgy, in which the love of the Lord, attested in the scriptures, judges his or her existence.

Can we not conceive of the ultimate encounter, the last judgment, with the same logic? This judgment is not a surprising sentence, imposed as it were from outside, and capable of being

The hidden power of the resurrection

In our last days, the event of Newness is the hidden power of the resurrection. Here we should reread all the texts of St Paul on this energy of the resurrection which from that time on is spreading in the world through the gospel. For us that means that in every event the incarnate Word, a new world, comes into our world of death. Jesus really died; but this invasion of the living God brings liberation from slavery for humanity, bound as it is in those multiple chains which are the devil, sin, death, the law, the flesh in the Pauline sense. The cross was the Hour of Newness: the eschaton, the age to come, has entered our time and dynamited all our tombs. This death is our resurrection. 'By the cross joy has spread throughout the world' (Byzantine Office of Easter, Sixth Ode).

The most urgent thing for us today is perhaps to discover what is the immeasurable greatness of his power in us who believe, 'according to the working of his great might, which he accomplished in Christ when he raised him from the dead' (Eph. 1.19–20).

Metropolitan Ignatius Hazim of Latakia, at the Uppsala Assembly of the World Council of Churches, 1968

rejected by the interested party, as in our courts. But in the light of Christ which has at last been made manifest, each individual judges himself or herself with a renewed conscience, from which illusions have been stripped away. In it, sin, long anaesthetized, will begin to cry out. There the spirit 'will judge the world over sin, justice and judgment' (John 16.8): that is to say that the Spirit of Christ will finally illuminate the true nature of sin; he will do justice to Christ and will bring to light the judgment which has been at work since the death and resurrection of Jesus.

Already today

For since Easter this sovereign judgment of Christ the Lord has already been exercised on all beings. 'As the Father has life in himself, so he has granted the Son also to have life in himself, and has given him authority to execute judgment because he is the Son of man' (John 5.26–27). The prince of this world has already been judged (16.11). But he who believes 'in eternal life does not come into judgment, but has passed from death to life' (5.24). The resurrection is already today; so it is now that judgment takes place.

And since we are risen, we must look on this ambiguous world from the perspective of the judgment of the Risen Christ. That is how discernment takes place. 'Moved by faith, the people of God tries to discern in the events, the needs and the longings which it shares with other men of our time, what may be genuine signs of the presence or the purpose of God' (Vatican II, *Gaudium et Spes*, 11.1). Thus for us eternal life, as we shall say at the end of this creed, is not only after tomorrow, in a future which is both attractive and disturbing; it is already a present: 'And this is eternal life, that they know thee the only true God, and Jesus Christ whom thou hast sent' (John 17.3).

The hope which makes us watchers awaiting the return of the master (see Matt. 25.1–13 and the other parables of vigilance) does not relieve us of our earthly tasks since it is already in this world that the kingdom of God must be able to take shape. This world is not a kind of waiting room for Christians, in which they seek to occupy themselves as best they can while waiting for a better world. Their world is an oratory and a laboratory, where our future is taking shape.

For we do not wait for the world to come passively, as one waits for a train. We expect it as a woman expects a child (John 16.21), giving it flesh of her flesh: it takes shape in her hope.

His kingdom will have no end

John the Baptist announced the kingdom of God as being very close (Mark 1.15). And Jesus himself took up this warning in his preaching: 'Repent, for the kingdom of God is at hand' (Matt. 4.17). Apparently, then, it is not his own reign that he announces but the reign of God, the kingdom of heaven.

However, through his words and above all his actions it seemed little by little to those who followed him that in him this kingdom had finally been inaugurated, a kingdom of peace, of justice, of victory over all forms of evil. It all happened as if he himself already represented the presence of this kingdom in person, to the point that those who asked him about it at the time of his trial could pretend to interpret this kingdom in a political sense with the intention of disturbing Pilate: 'He forbids us to pay tribute to Caesar and says that he is Christ a king' (Luke 23.2). John reminds us how Jesus must have set people right: 'My kingdom is not of this world' (John 18.36). It was important to recognize that his kingdom and the kingdom of God are one; by him and in him God inaugurates this new world in which he is finally master. Pilate was its unconscious herald when he had the royal status of Jesus of Nazareth proclaimed in all the languages of the realm in the placard on the cross (John 19.19–22).

St Paul, for whom the complete inauguration of this kingdom still remains a hope, announces the end of time as the work of Christ inaugurating the kingdom of God, his Father, by his definitive triumph over evil and death. 'Then

---

Thy kingdom come!

As our Lord and Saviour has said, the kingdom comes without our noticing it. One cannot say, 'It is there, it is here,' or even, 'There it is.' For the kingdom of God is among you. And in fact this word is very near to us; it is in our mouth and in our heart. In this case it is evident that the one who prays for the coming of the kingdom of God is right to pray that this kingdom of God should germinate, bear fruit and find fulfilment in him. Among all the saints in whom God reigns and who obey his spiritual laws, he lives as in a well-organized city. Christ is present in him and Christ reigns with the Father in this perfect soul, according to his saying: 'We shall come and dwell with him, we shall make our home with him.'

The kingdom of God which is in us, when we continue to progress, will arrive at its perfection when the word of the Apostle is fulfilled: the Christ, having subjected all his enemies, will hand back his royal power to God the Father that God may be all in all. That is why, praying without ceasing, with dispositions divinized by the Word, we say, 'Our Father who art in heaven, hallowed be thy name, thy kingdom come.'

Origen (c.185–253), *On Prayer*. Roman office of readings for the festival of Christ the King of the Universe

comes the end, when he delivers the kingdom to God the Father after destroying every rule and every authority and power. For he must reign until he has put all his enemies under his feet' (I Cor. 15.24–25, citing Ps. 110.1). It is this reign of God and his Christ which will have no end.

It was ironically said: 'Jesus proclaimed the kingdom of God and the church came.' One can be struck by the apparent difference between the complexity of the church organization which has been set up over the ages and the preaching of Jesus with his rustic parables. But in welcoming the Spirit of Jesus and the logic of his incarnation the Christian communities simply sought to inscribe the demands of the gospel on each age of the history of the peoples. The church of the disciples does not claim to be the kingdom in its ultimate realization. But it knows that it can already see something of it, and it wants to be the sign, the sacrament, the legible and effective announcement that it has begun to come since Pentecost. Every time Christians gather to celebrate the eucharist in memory of the death and resurrection of Jesus, the kingdom of God, in his Christ, takes shape in their life. This is the source of the conversion of their everyday existence. In the logic of eucharistic sharing they have their own way of looking at family and social life, work and leisure, responsibility, the excercise of power and sexuality, the humanization of relationships between individuals and peoples. The kingdom is already the whole of this life transfigured by the love of the Trinity. In seeing the life of those who recite the creed one should be able to recognize even now the first light of this kingdom which will have no end.

Reign and kingdom of God

Reign and kingdom translate the same Greek word in the New Testament and the same Hebrew word in the Old Testament. The reign of God is his sovereignty as it will be recognized by all men and women on the day of salvation. It tends to be translated by kingdom where the text suggests its specific realization in space: one is then invited to enter it, to take a place in it, to dwell in it.

Israel sang that God reigns even now (Ps. 93.1–2; 99.1–4; 145.11–13) while awaiting the day when this kingdom would be manifested in human history. For the New Testament writers the work of Jesus in his preaching, his fight against sickness and against the powers of evil, his death and resurrection, are the triumphal fulfilment of this kingdom.

Matthew, respecting the Jewish usage which avoids pronouncing the name of God, speaks of the kingdom of heaven (e.g. in 3.2), not to suggest that it is far away in heaven but to stress that the one who reigns here and now is the Father who is in heaven.

PART THREE

18 I Believe in the Holy Spirit

When Paul arrived at Ephesus, the few disciples that he met told him that they had never heard of the Holy Spirit. They were not unaware of his existence because the Old Testament mentions him. But they had had no experience of his active presence. Would it be an exaggeration to say that two thousand years afterwards Paul would receive the same reply?

However, our perception of the Spirit is often very confused. We do not know what to call him. We do not know how to represent him. Metaphors only represent one aspect of his manifestations. They would make him breath, fire, wind, dove, living water, seal.

A presence to recognize

A mysterious and active presence, he is recognized by his well-tried effects. His action seems manifest to the eyes of believers, yet recognizing him is a real act of faith.

A quick look at the most personalized confessions of faith show us a real need. For the Spirit, there is often substituted a faith in humanity the creative capacities of which are emphasized to the point of saying that humanity is the summit of the universe and that everything has been put in our hands. Should we see the influence of modern philosophy in this shift? Or does this

Spirit

When we speak of spirit, when we say that God is spirit, what do we mean?

The Hebrew term *ruach* is usually translated by the Greek *pneuma*. It denotes breath, air, wind, soul. The 379 instances of the term in the Old Testament can be divided into three groups of equal importance.

– Ruach is primarily the wind (Ps. 18.11). This wind disturbs the waters from which creation emerges. A cosmic reality, the wind is an instrument of God which makes the winds his messengers (Ps. 104.4).

– The ruach-wind is human breath, the air that we breathe; his presence is a sign of life; when the wind blows on the dry bones breath

returns to them and they live (Ezek. 37). The absence of ruach is a sign of death; when their breath goes, people die (Ps. 146.4). The principle of human life, this breath-wind denotes every force which drives people to act.

– More particularly, ruach is the breath which comes forth from the mouth of God, his living power (Ps. 33.6). It raised up the prophets. It is also given to kings, to Yahweh's anointed (Isa. 11.2).

John stresses this Spirit which works in and through Jesus. He is the Paraclete, the defender, who will be given to the disciples with the breath of Pentecost morning.

stress on human dignity show the necessary foundation of any affirmation about the action of God today?

The fact remains that the words for speaking about the Spirit do not come easily. The Spirit seems to many people to be a subsidiary reality, a way of speaking, an impersonal force.

The expression of this recognition

Scripture and the prayer of the church refer to the specific action of the Spirit at a very early stage. And yet the construction of this third part of the creed does not indicate an immediate coherence. It seems more like a catalogue than a well-wrought argument. However, we shall see how this third panel of the triptych gives the creed its *raison d'être*, its framework of expression, its scope and without doubt also its limit. It is from the same movement that we are invited to read the third part of the creed. There is a close link between the brief affirmation of our faith in the Holy Spirit and a group of realities that we recognize subsequently to be the works of the Spirit.

This unity is clearly affirmed in the Apostles' Creed: 'I believe in the Holy Spirit, the Holy Catholic Church, the communion of saints, the forgiveness of sins, the resurrection of the body, and the life everlasting.'

To give a better indication that the totality of the believing architecture of the creed presupposes the action of the Spirit, numerous groups of Christians study it across the grain, seeing it successively as an affirmation by the church in the power of the Spirit, a confession of the lordship of Jesus, the crucified one whom God raised, and a recognition, of the oneness of God the Father and Creator.

The faith of the Church

If we do this, we get a better idea of the movement of faith and its ecclesial character. The faith professed is that of the Church, a treasure which tradition hands down to us, the fruit of the contemplation of the mystery and a difficult way of giving clear expression to this certainty of faith. Words always translate and betray experience.

The Church is not, strictly speaking, an object of faith. It is rather the unique subject of the creed. It confesses that it receives itself from a God who is Father, Son and Spirit. It is not said that we believe in the Church any more than we believe in any of the other works of God. We proclaim our faith in the Church, that is to say in its existence, its supernatural reality, its unity. We profess that the Church is formed by the Holy Spirit, that it is the proper work of the Spirit, the instrument by which he sanctifies us. Our membership of the Church and our participation in its life are to be experienced in this power and this freedom of the Spirit.

To believe in the Holy Spirit is to hold that God acts ceaselessly. This God of Abraham, of Isaac and of Jacob, this God of Jesus of Nazareth, reveals himself in a history. He has not ceased to express himself in human history; he has not ceased to express himself in human words: the Spirit manifests the passion that God has for his creation. He involves himself in a covenant which gives human beings responsibility. The confession of the Holy Spirit denotes the transcendence of the encounter between God and humanity: if believers are before God they are also in God. They have the experience of a God who is more intimate to them than they are to themselves. The temptation to dualism is a reflex action for believers. The affirmation of the action of the Spirit involves human beings in a historical responsibility.

Thus at the heart of the Christian act of faith the Holy Spirit is more often felt than explained. He is a power, this force from on high which Christ promised to his disciples. He is the power of the Most High which takes Mary under his shadow (Luke 1.35). He is this power sent from

God by Christ so that the good news may be announced to all nations. In receiving it the apostles are given their mission to witness to the resurrection of Christ.

The gift of the Spirit was made on the morning of Pentecost under the signs of wind and fire: the wind which blows where it wills and of which no one knows whence it comes or whither it goes and the fire of the burning bush which burns without being consumed (Ex. 3.2), but also the fire which purifies and tests the gold in the furnace.

The event of Pentecost

As it is described to us in the Acts of the Apostles, the irruption of the Spirit is basically disturbing. These men who for the most part were remote from Jesus at the decisive moment, these men whom the risen Christ had sent back to their everyday tasks, felt the irresistible need to proclaim in the city of Jerusalem that God had raised Jesus of Nazareth and that they were his witnesses. The public announcement inaugurates the last times (eschatology) as if the messianic times had come. The reference to the prophet Joel is significant:

And in the last days it shall be, God declares,
that I will pour out my Spirit upon all flesh,
and your sons and daughters shall prophesy,
and your young men shall see visions,
and your old men shall dream dreams.
Yes, and on my menservants and my
    maidservants in those days
I will pour out my Spirit (Acts 2.17–18).

Peter, who had not wanted to have anything to do with Jesus of Nazareth on the day of his arrest, becomes the one who proclaims the action of God. For him, only the gift of the Spirit can explain the miracle of which his audience are witnesses.

If he gives the gift of languages, the Spirit is primarily the one who allows people to affirm

the resurrection of Christ. 'Let all the house of Israel therefore know assuredly that God has made him both Lord and Christ, this Jesus whom you crucified' (Acts 2.36).

Thus the resurrection of Jesus Christ takes its place in a complex that one could describe logically; the event is no longer only historical; it signifies the irruption of a new time in which God alone has the initiative. Each one, moreover, finds his proper identity and can understand the marvels of God in his language, in his culture.

When the event becomes advent

This Pentecost which gives its whole dimension to the event of Easter is to become the matrix of the whole mystical experience of Christianity. All the conversion stories mention a breaking in the Spirit, in which each person seeks to grasp after having been grasped.

The fundamental event becomes a watershed. This disconcerting transition proves to be a point of reference for existence. Paul finds the need to repeat his own experience on the Damascus road three times. However, these irruptions of grace must not lead us to stress the overwhelming character of all spiritual experience. Many people in all good faith bear witness to an action by the Holy Spirit which takes place in a slow, misty progress. It nevertheless remains the case that the truth of this fundamental event only stands out completely at a time of discernment, a time of looking back on life, of recall.

The Church's work of commemoration (*anamnesis*) is already present in Peter's long discourse on the morning of Pentecost. But it is described more exactly in the story of the pilgrims on the Emmaus road in the Gospel of Luke (24.13–35).

We have here what amounts to a catechesis of the first Christian communities, as they re-read events in the light of the Law and the Prophets; as in the breaking of bread in memory of him, Christ reveals himself.

The texts of the Gospels are important evi-

dence of the spiritual approach which consists in commemorating in order to illuminate and understand the break-through of radical newness. This newness, a sign of God's gift, can only be welcomed as a manifestation of God's faithfulness to his covenant plan.

An enthusiastic asceticism, this path of anamnesis led the first Christians to be ready to enter actively into the time of waiting, taking history seriously.

The experience of the gift and reception of receiving the Spirit which the first Christian communities encountered had led them to confess its active presence. They were not concerned to define it. And yet scripture is already full of more specific definitions which would serve, especially in the fourth century, to describe the Spirit and proclaim his divinity against the heretics.

Pentecost.
Manuscript of the monks of Helmarshausen, twelfth century.
Photo coll. part. D. R

19   He is Lord

The Council of Nicaea (325) had clearly affirmed the divinity of the Son against the Arians. It made only a brief mention of the Holy Spirit. It was for the Council of Constantinople (381) to name the Spirit Holy, Lord and Giver of life.

To say that the Spirit is Lord is to recognize that he is not a creature, that his mission cannot be compared with that of the angels, ministers of God. He is not only a force coming from God, he is a divine Person. Like the Son, the Spirit is called Lord (Kyrios), but the Greek texts of the creed of Constantinople use the article in the neuter, and not in the masculine, as with the Father. This could be translated by 'that which is in the category of Lord'. As Athanasius put it: 'So the Spirit was among the people, it was God who, by the Son in the Spirit, was among them.'

Not only a force but a Person

Because he is a divine Person, the Spirit makes us participate in the life of God. 'By this we know that we abide in him and he in us, because he has given us of his own Spirit' (I John 4.13). It is the Greek fathers who demonstrate the divinity of the Spirit, going back from effects to cause. The sanctification brought out by baptism can only be attributed to a being who is himself the source of sanctification, for he is the holy God.

Just as it is by the Son that we know the Father, so too we know him in the Spirit. He gives us access to the mystery of the Trinity by conforming us to the image of the Son. St Paul said to the Christians in Thessalonica: 'May the Lord direct your hearts to the love of God and to the steadfastness of Christ' (II Thess. 3.5).

Unlike the Son, the Spirit is not begotten. He proceeds from the Father and participates in his glory. The Spirit is equally Lord in his role of sanctifying the world. He fills the universe. We can even talk of cosmic stakes, since even now the creation groans in the pangs of childbirth. The active presence of the Spirit invites us to a better understanding of the worth of the world. This world entrusted to human responsibility is also that which is brought to birth by the Spirit of God.

The Spirit at work

'Your Spirit works in human hearts and enemies finally talk, adversaries extend their hands, people in opposition agree to go part of the way together' (Preface to the Second Eucharistic Prayer for Reconciliation). The Spirit is at work and guides the combat of love in the name of God's faithfulness. Christians do not have a monopoly in the action of the Spirit and nothing can limit him in his action. Moreover, the Church must continually be able to read his activity, and recognize him in his ineffable presence and his transforming power. Fortunately we have rediscovered that this is one of the primordial tasks of all mission: to be able to read the presence of the Spirit which goes before us and to be able to give thanks for his initiative. Too often we believe that the Holy Spirit is in our baggage, lagging behind our methods of evangelization.

Vatican II reminds us that 'at all times the Church carries the responsibility of reading the signs of the time and of interpreting them in the light of the Gospel, if it is to carry out its task. In language intelligible to every generation, she should be able to answer the ever-recurring questions which men ask about the meaning of this present life and of the life to come, and how one is related to the other' (*Lumen Gentium* 4).

Reading the signs of the times is a matter of recognizing that the Spirit goes before us, that he has the initiative. But it is also a matter of accepting a real autonomy and an authentic appositeness of the world in its own development. The world is this creation willed by the Lord in which the Spirit is at work.

This better understanding of the world has allowed the Church to have a better position in relationship to it. Not in competition, as if one had to reject the world! But as the sphere in which the Church had to advance, poor and as a servant. So the Church of the Council recognizes that it makes a contribution to the world but that it also receives from this world.

The Spirit and history

At work in the world, the Spirit labours on with human history. He invites us to dwell in this history. He also invites us to be its agents. History must not be experienced as an endless cycle or as an inexorable destiny. The fatalism which too often marks the relationship of human beings to their history can be overcome when the believer discovers that determinism is not everything. The Spirit who goes about his work in the world makes human history the place of the coming of the kingdom. He opens history to creative newness in the horizon of the kingdom.

In the form of a dove

The dove was not a symbol of the Spirit in the Old Testament or the rabbinical writings. Need we look for a different meaning from that of a pair of wings showing that a gift comes from heaven? The gift of the Spirit to the prophets was sometimes represented by a winged heavenly messenger. The dove was a messenger and the message was given in heavenly words (*bath-qol*). The dove was, however, a symbol of Israel, the chosen people. It may therefore be a representation or the symbolic presence of that people and the penitential movement with which Jesus wanted to be at one, since he was the new Adam and represented and embodied the new people of God (Matt. 3.14–15). In addition, the titles 'Son of God' and 'Servant' were also applied to the whole people of God. The dove might therefore represent it as the people to whom the Spirit was to come through the Messiah.

In the Christian tradition the dove was to be the symbol of the Holy Spirit. This is clear from iconographical evidence and from a whole series of texts, including liturgical ones. The part played in Augustine's ecclesiology by *columba* is well known – it is a name for the one, holy Church and for the Holy Spirit.

We should also note that it is forbidden to represent the Holy Spirit in human form. The divine Persons may be represented only under the aspects attested by scripture (*Decree of the Holy Office*, 16 March 1928), like the dove or the tongues of fire, or the finger of God. In the East, by adaptation to theological needs at different times, the Holy Spirit was represented in the form of a dove, tongues of fire, light, luminous aura, ray, etc. and in a human form: the three magi, the three guests of Abraham (Andrei Rublev) and by geometric schematization.

Y. Congar, *I Believe in the Holy Spirit* I, Geoffrey Chapman and Seabury Press 1983, pp.16f.

Pentecost.
Evangeliary of
Cologne, 1250.
Photo private
collection

He is there first and calls. He overturns, sends, brings growth and liberation. In a world which is too horizontal and too much the prisoner of its contradictions, he introduces a critical dynamism.

The presence of the Spirit cannot be discerned naively. If it is, it risks being no more than a self-justification. The church invites us to discernment. As St John says, 'He will convince the world of sin and of righteousness and of judgment' (John 16.8). If they have not withdrawn from the world, the disciples are invited not to be of the world. They cannot purely and simply endorse the values of the world. In the name of his involvement in the world, the believer is constantly invited to judge, to take a distance so as to be able to act better. 'Do not be conformed to this world but be transformed by the renewal of your mind, that you may prove what is the will of God, what is good and acceptable and perfect' (Rom. 12.2).

20   He Gives Life

The Spirit which hovered over the waters in the beginning is seen as the Creator's breath of life. By his breathing God gives life. The presence of the Spirit was seen by the Hebrews as the life-giving presence of God in humanity. God gives life. Moreover this certainty led them to say that since his life brings life to humanity, when it disappears, they die. In their faith the Hebrews therefore came to say, in a kind of shorthand: God gives both life and death. But God is also the one who can give new life. We know the great vision of the dry bones in the book of the prophet Ezekiel: 'Come from the four winds, o breath, and breathe upon these slain, that they may live. So I prophesied as he commanded me, and the breath came into them, and they lived, and stood upon their feet, an exceeding great host' (37.9–10).

It was as a daughter of Israel that Mary had the fertile experience of the coming of the Spirit. He who is the source of life came to her, to leave in her the germ of all life. By being open to the Word of God, Mary accepts the irruption of the power of God in her life. Her song of thanksgiving well expresses the degree to which she recapitulates the hope of Israel and also the degree to which she represents the gift of God to humanity: 'From henceforth all generations will call me blessed.'

The Spirit present in Jesus

This fertile power of the Spirit also intervenes in the story of the baptism of Jesus. In the form of a dove, the Spirit descends on him and a voice says, 'You are my well-beloved Son, this day have I begotten you.' Filled with the Holy Spirit, Jesus will be led through the wilderness, all through his life up to the cross.

The Gospel of Luke mentions the Spirit far more than the other Synoptic Gospels. With John, Luke is the one who expresses most clearly how the mission of Christ is entirely in the power of the Spirit, the source of life. So Christ can say: 'I come that they may have life, and have it abundantly' (John 10.10).

Up to the passion, the Spirit is the bond of communion between the Father and the Son. At the point of dying, the Son exclaims in a great cry, 'Father, into thy hands I commend my Spirit' (Luke 23.46).

This same Spirit that Christ hands over in an act of total love is the one who, through the resurrection, enables him to participate fully in the glory of the Father. Then the Christ can send forth the Holy Spirit as he had promised. The disciples are no longer orphans. They discover that they are adopted sons and in turn can call God Father.

'It is the Spirit himself bearing witness with our spirit that we are children of God, and if children, then heirs, heirs of God and fellow-heirs with Christ' (Rom. 8.16–17). The Spirit gives life because he makes us leave the shores of fear. He brings to the remembrance of the disciples all that Jesus of Nazareth had said to them.

He leads into all truth

By allowing themselves to be worked on by the Spirit, believers can hope to see the plan of love

Figure praying. Third-century fresco. Catacombs of Rome.
Photo Private collection

devised by the one who does not cease to say, 'Your thoughts are not my thoughts and my ways are not your ways' (Isa. 55.8). Made fruitful by the Holy Spirit, the believer recognizes a logic of giving birth at work in him. He has the experience of freedom by participation in the divine life. The Christian experiences this path of divinization by being crucified with Christ: 'It is no longer I who live,' says St Paul, 'but Christ who lives in me, and the life I now live in the flesh I live by faith in the Son of God, who loved me and gave himself for me' (Gal. 2.20).

The gift of the Spirit comes to perfect the work of the divine inbreathing because 'it is the Spirit which gives life, the flesh is of no avail' (John 6.63). Life thus given in abundance leads the believer to restate the conviction of the psalm: 'Thou art fearful and wonderful: Wonderful are thy works' (Ps. 139.14). Moreover St Irenaeus could write that the glory of God is living humanity.

Nothing leads us to have suspicions about the incarnate condition of humankind. On the contrary, there are numerous passages in the Gospels which, on the contrary, invite us to take it seriously. The Spirit does not call on us to flee the human condition but to experience it in the name of the divine plan which is revealed to us by Jesus Christ in his fullness.

The signs of the kingdom

Following Jesus of Nazareth, the Spirit calls on us to experience the signs of the kingdom today: 'The Spirit of the Lord is upon me, because he has anointed me to preach good news to the poor. He has sent me to proclaim release to the captives and the recovering of sight to the blind, to set at liberty those who are oppressed, to proclaim the acceptable year of the Lord' (Luke 4.18).

These signs of the kingdom are in our hands; they speak today of the lifegiving activity of God. They go far beyond the sacramental signs and give each individual a prophetic responsibility. Are we not called to read as a sign of the Spirit all that leads to more humanity, brotherhood and solidarity? The Spirit blows where it wills and we do not own it. On the other hand, to bear witness to a Spirit which gives life will always be to involve oneself in the discipleship of Christ by specific actions in the risk of not being understood. The servant is not greater than the master, and for many people today to follow Christ means sacrificing their own lives. Commitment to the poorest and the least significant is the principal way which the witness to Christ will take. In turn he becomes the one who sows the seeds of life. He can say again that the breath of the life of God and the fire of his presence will make all things new. Thus the Spirit makes the universe created by the word of God blossom forth. It gives everything its full growth, its full maturity.

But we need to go further. The power of the Spirit is also at work in our lives as the seed of life which has no end. The fathers of the church speak of 'seeds of immortality'. The gift of God overturns the contingences of our bodily experience. The Spirit is the life-principle for the resurrection of the flesh, as we shall see. So it is that the third baptismal question of the Apostolic Tradition of Hippolytus is put like this: 'Do you believe in the Holy Spirit, in the Holy Church, for the resurrection of the flesh?'

21 Life according to the Spirit

In the Letter to the Galatians, Paul affirms; 'If we live by the Spirit, let us also walk by the Spirit' (5.25). This Spirit which makes men and women free because he frees them from temptation and sin is a 'personalizing' force in every believer.

To live according to the Spirit is to allow oneself to be modelled on the Word of God, like clay in the hands of the potter. It is not easy to recognize this dependence and to make it the place of our freedom. There is a strong temptation nowadays to absolutize autonomy, which leads us to say 'I owe nothing to anyone.' Christ overcame the tempter to the degree that he affirms that his existence is completely one of obedience to the Father. This obedience, this attentive listening to the word of God, was already present in the law of Moses: 'Hear, O Israel, the salutes and the ordinances which I speak in your hearing this day, and you shall learn them and be careful to do them' (Deut. 5.1).

But the law was eternal and Jeremiah had prophesied: 'I will put my law within them, and I will write it upon their hearts; and I will be their God, and they shall be my people' (31.33). The new law is an internal one. It realizes in us the gift of the Spirit promised to the Messiah: 'And the Spirit of the Lord shall rest upon him, the spirit of wisdom and understanding, the spirit of counsel and might, the spirit of knowledge and the fear of Yahweh' (Isa. 11.2). This list, to which piety was later to be added in the Middle Ages, is the list of the seven gifts of the Holy Spirit.

The Spirit of the Risen Christ which is given in the rite of baptism introduces the believer into a movement of death and resurrection which lasts all his life; life under the sign of birth, of giving birth, but also of exodus and suffering. Paul writes to the Colossians: 'For you have died, and your life is hid with Christ in God. Christ who is our life appears, then you also will appear with him in glory' (3.3–4).

The fruit of the Spirit

Overwhelmed by the Spirit, those who have been baptized have the experience of this new life which slowly will make the 'old man' die in them. They live from the fruit of the Spirit which is 'love, joy, peace, patience, kindness, goodness, faithfulness, gentleness self-control' (Gal. 5.22–23).

The Spirit sets the love of God in the hearts of believers. This love is primarily recognition of the prevenient initiative of the Father. Only the contemplation of the love of God which is manifested to the extent of the humility of Christ's death on the cross can help us to understand Paul's affirmation 'Love never fails' (I Cor. 13.8). In proclaiming that, the apostle is not speaking of the quality of our human links; he is meditating on the intensity of communion between the Father and the Son. This stress on love must not be seen as an easier way. Love thus set at the heart of the act of faith is the radiant energy of the mystery of God. Love alone is worthy of faith, worthy of involving the whole of a human life. Love understood in this way is no longer the expression of our sensibility but is the echo of the life of the Trinity. Did not St Bernard speak of the Spirit as the kiss between the Father and the Son?

If love comes first, joy is its manifestation.

Christians repeat the actions of Christ. Scene from the life of St Casternsis. Mosaic of the Cathedral of Monreale. End of twelfth century. Photo private collection

When the Spirit presides over the meeting between Mary and her cousin Elizabeth, Mary sings of her joy and magnifies the Lord. Similarly, confronted with the joy of his disciples as they return from their first mission, Jesus exults under the action of the Spirit (Luke 10.21).

This joy is the source of every act of thanksgiving and we have too often forgotten that nothing can take it from us. The eucharistic sacrifice must be steeped in this joy and praise. Christian communities still have some way to go before they are these assemblies celebrating the action of God in a significant way.

All that Christ has told us about his relationship to the Father and his saving mission is aimed at enabling us to share in his joy that our joy may be full (John 15.11). Thus for a Christian joy has the status of an imperative. Paul repeats 'Rejoice!' four times. This joy cannot be the transient state of someone who remains on the

118

surface of things: it is the expression of the life of God which shines forth where it has taken root. Do Christians know that they are the tabernacles of the joy of God?

However, this joy can be truly expressed only when the suffering of humanity is fully shared. Then the roads of liberation become places of effective solidarity. 'For the creation waits with eager longing for the revealing of the sons of God' (Rom. 8.19). It would even be indecent for believers to show their joy without experiencing a real compassion for all those who suffer in body or spirit, and even without becoming actively involved in the struggle against all that which deeply wounds men and women.

The seven gifts of the Spirit

The source of the theology of the gifts is the text from Isaiah:

There shall come forth a shoot from the stump of Jesse,
and a branch shall go out of his roots.
And the spirit of Yahweh shall rest upon him,
the spirit of wisdom and understanding,
the spirit of counsel and might,
the spirit of knowledge and the fear of the Lord.
And his delight shall be in the fear of the Lord
(11.1–2).

The Middle Ages experienced a great theological development in the symbolism of the figure seven, already attested in St Irenaeus. These gifts of the Holy Spirit which came to represent the theological virtues invite us to be guided by the Lord. St Thomas Aquinas sought to relate these gifts to the virtues and the beatitudes. Beyond the enumeration of the seven gifts, the spiritual tradition invites us to recognize that we cannot respond to the call for sanctification without entrusting ourselves to the grace of God which calls for a continual renunciation of our sufficiency. The understanding of the faith leads to prayer and humility, so that 'Let him who boasts, boast of the Lord' (I Cor. 1.31).

The Spirit is the active memory of Christians

The Spirit not only has to be discovered but is primarily that by which we dare to believe. The Spirit of wisdom and revelation, it gives us knowledge of the Father. It allows us to recognize grace as grace. It is the subjective possibility of revelation. It is that which allows us to receive and welcome the word of God. The Spirit alone allows us to confess that Jesus is Lord. Thus faith is primarily a matter of being open to the action of God (a theological virtue).

We can understand why the author of the Letter to the Ephesians writes: 'May the Spirit open the eyes of your hearts, that you may know what is the hope to which he has called you, what are the riches of his glorious inheritance in the saints, and what is the immeasurable greatness of his power in us who believe according to the working of his great might, which he accomplished in Christ' (1.18–19). The Spirit stirs the memory of the believer. He does not teach anything new and constantly refers to Christ – the Word of God. 'The Holy Spirit whom the Father will send in my name, he will teach you all things, and bring to your remembrance all that I have told you' (John 14.26). Thus the believer is no longer a servant but a friend of God, since it has been granted to him or her to know the mystery of God, even as he or she can be known.

So every relationship with God is marked by the Holy Spirit. Christian prayer is prayer in the Spirit, inspired by God. The words matter less than being open to his presence. Only the Spirit can lead you to say, 'Abba, Father, Lord, open my lips and my mouth shall show forth thy praise,' as we say each day. We pray to the one who knows what we need without our asking him. But in this way our prayer produces in us the desire to welcome the gift of God. In the Spirit and through Christ, all Christian prayer is addressed to the Father and opens our hearts to the relationship of love between the divine persons. How many believers have found difficulty in praying because they think of their prayer in terms of their capacity for expressing it. To pray in the Spirit is to allow ourselves to be guided in our relationship to God by his desire. It is to listen to his Word and discover there the breath which supports it.

The theological and cardinal virtues

'He who raised Christ Jesus from the dead will give life to your mortal bodies also through his Spirit which dwells in you' (Rom. 8.11).

Sanctifying grace, which makes the believer the temple of the Spirit, is involved in various gifts.

Persons who are in the process of realization discover that they can only become what they are destined to be on the basis of something that is already given. In faith, we discover this God who is more intimate to us than we are to ourselves. We recognize that 'Faith, Hope, Love' are gifts of God, But we also recognize that these virtues direct us towards God, that they have God as their object. In this sense they are called theological virtues. We should remember that in the Letter to the Corinthians Paul subordinates them all to love.

This term virtue, the force of which is not always seen today, is also used in speaking of moral action. It can be seen as the habitual disposition which inclines a person to do good. The theological tradition, taking up the heritage of the Greek philosophers, speaks of four cardinal virtues: prudence, justice, fortitude and temperance. These moral virtues orientate our will towards moral progress, putting us at the disposal of the divine action. Far from introducing a morality based on duty, the virtues endorse human development as welcoming God's gift.

22 He Proceeds from the Father and the Son

We have seen how important it was to indicate that the Spirit was not just a power coming from God, a means of sanctification. Calling him Holy and Lord also leads us to indicate his participation in the divine life. If being with the Lord Jesus from his baptism to the day when he was taken up allowed his followers to affirm his personal reality, the same thing goes for the Spirit.

The whole of Jesus' life bears witness that the Spirit comes from the Father. 'You know how God anointed Jesus of Nazareth with the holy Spirit and with power; how he went about doing good and healing all that were oppressed by the devil; for God was with him' (Acts 10.38). Similarly, it was clear for the disciples that the mission which the Father entrusted to the Spirit was to bear witness. 'When the Paraclete comes, whom I shall send to you from the Father, even the Spirit of truth, who proceeds from the Father, he will bear witness to me' (John 15.26).

Of the same nature as the Father

We must go further and recognize that to say of the Spirit that he proceeds from the Father is tantamount to confessing the identity of nature between the Spirit and the Father, just as the term 'begotten' stresses the identity of nature between the Father and the Son. The Spirit himself is not created. As St Basil (died 379) says: 'The Spirit proceeds from the Father by the Son'. The Council of Constantinople did not go further than that. It did not link the Spirit with the Son while according him the same glory as the Father and the Son. Theological thinking met up with the liturgical expression of the prayers of the church in a communal glorification. These doxologies, of which we find the echo in the texts of the New Testament, are the first traces of a trinitarian affirmation.

In fact, with the description of the Spirit as a divine Person, the God of the biblical revelation proved to be a communion of Persons. For some, the time of the manifestation of the Spirit seemed to follow after the time of the incarnation. We

---

'Economic' Trinity and 'immanent' Trinity

The Trinity is a mystery of salvation. Otherwise it would not be revealed. The Trinity as it manifests itself in the economy or the history of salvation is called the economic Trinity. Jesus is not simply God, he is the Son; his second divine person, the Logos of God, is man; he and only he.

Life within the divine Trinity is called the immanent Trinity. The theory of Karl Rahner (the famous German theologian who died recently) states that the economic Trinity is immanent Trinity and vice versa. God makes himself known by communicating himself. And yet are we not invited to believe that the full and entire communication of the mystery of the Trinity will be revealed only at the end of time?

periodically find this heretical temptation in the history of the church, a trend which was to be developed by Joachim di Fiore in the Middle Ages. For others, like Irenaeus, Christ and the Spirit are the two manifestations of the love of God: the two hands of God.

The Spirit of the Son

Since the Holy Spirit had been confessed as a divine Person, it was important to specify his relationship with the only Son. He could not be another begotten Son. Moreover the Father, logically, had to remain the absolute and unique origin of the life of the Trinity.

Theological cultures, language and sensibilities led the West and the East to express these relations between the divine Persons in different ways. Without going into detail, we might remember that the East was more concerned to manifest the monarchy of the Father, the only being without an origin who remained the source of the life of the Trinity. The West developed more specifically the relations between the divine Persons, expressing them in terms of shared love. Each confessed that it is the Spirit of Christ which is given, and that the Spirit is disseminated because the Son participates in the glory of the Father.

A controversial affirmation

The introduction of the expression *Filioque* (and from the Son) into the Creed crystallized some profound tensions. In fact the Council of Ephesus had prohibited any modification to the text produced by the Council and the term was used in a unilateral way in the course of certain celebrations in the West. To begin with, its rejection by the East was more canonical than theological. It was one more argument in the schism which came about in 1054.

For the Council of Lyons (1274), 'The Spirit proceeds eternally from the Father and the Son, not from two principles but from one and the same principle, not by two spirations but by a single spiration.' Over and above the disputes over interpretation, one formula would seem to be held in common: the Spirit comes from the Father by the Son. The unique element is the breath of life which manifests the bond of love between the divine Persons.

The life of the Trinity can be contemplated in the communion of Persons as expressed so perfectly by Rublev's icon of the Trinity. The three persons have such similar faces that interpreters hesitate, not to say differ, over the identification of the Persons. But the life of the Trinity can also be discovered in its historical manifestation (there was talk of the 'economic Trinity') in which humanity and all creation are caught up in an endless movement of love.

Icon of the Trinity.
Andrei Rublev,
fifteenth century.
Photo Mandel-Ziolo

123

23   He has Spoken by the Prophets

The attribution of the gift of prophecy to the Spirit is a theme common to all holy scripture. In his prayer, Peter thanks God by saying to him, 'By the mouth of our father David, thy servant, thou didst say by the Holy Spirit . . .' (Acts 4.25). The Spirit led the people of God towards messianic salvation through the mediation of the prophets. Each in his own way could have said, as did Jeremiah, 'I did not know how to speak, I am a child.' The prophet is a witness to the faithfulness of God. Like a shepherd, God leads his people to rest through his spirit, but 'they rebelled and grieved his Holy Spirit' (Isa. 63.10).

The author of the Letter to the Hebrews could say, 'In many and various ways God spoke of old to our fathers by the prophets; but in these last days he has spoken to us by a Son, whom he appointed the heir of all things, through whom also he created the world' (Heb. 1.1). The birth of John the Baptist is hailed by his father Zechariah in a prophecy which is a turning point between the old covenant and the new. To begin with he gives thanks for the salvation 'announced by the mouth of his holy prophets in former times', and then he paints a vision of the future relating to the mission of his son. Also in Luke's Gospel, the old Simeon blesses God, for his eyes have seen the salvation prepared before the face of all people.

Jesus of Nazareth takes his place in this long prophetic line. He knows that Jerusalem kills its prophets (Luke 13.34) and, while recognizing the cause, deliberately goes up to the city of David. He takes upon himself all the hope and the intransigence of the prophets to bear witness to the faithfulness of God his Father.

The Spirit in scripture

History itself is recognized as the history of the manifestation of the creative and redemptive action of God in the power of the Spirit. It has that character precisely because it is a history of salvation, a history of the desire for a covenant with God.

It is within this broad horizon that one can speak of the inspiration of the scriptures. The texts of both the Old and the New Testament bear witness to the welcome given in faith to revelation. Moreover one can only speak of revelation in faith, where revelation is seen as the word of God which reaches human hearts. So the word of God and the holy Spirit are linked. Scripture is alive only in the stream of tradition which is broader than scripture itself. The strongest affirmation of the inspiration of scripture appears in II Timothy: 'All scripture is inspired by God and profitable for teaching, for reproof, for correction and for training in righteousness, that the man of God may be complete, equipped for every good work' (3.16–17). So the scriptures have the power to communicate the wisdom which leads to salvation by faith. However, 'no prophecy of scripture is a matter of one's own interpretation' (II Peter 1.20). Supported by the faith of the church, scripture becomes the sacramental place where revelation is received. It is the obligatory point of transition in the relationship with the God of revelation.

Moved by the Holy Spirit, men and women have spoken of God's part. Their words and their writings are stamped by their culture: 'the interpreter of sacred Scriptures, if he is to ascertain what God has wished to communicate to us, should carefully search out the meaning which the sacred writers really had in mind, that meaning which God had thought well to manifest through the medium of their words' (*Dei Verbum*, 12). The interpretation of the scriptures is a responsibility entrusted to the Church in the name of the whole of the living tradition which supports it and gives it life. It is the Church which has decided to recognize one scripture and not another.

The prophets today

Has inspiration come to an end? If we talk of the closing of revelation after the death of the last apostle, does that mean that the time of inspiration lies behind us? That is not the case. The breath of the Spirit is present when believers meditate on scripture, when they interpret it and give it flesh in their own lives. This work of interpretation, which is always difficult, takes place in a dialogue in the church. In fact we must

---

Who is a prophet?

There are numerous and varied prophets through the Old Testament. In the book of Deuteronomy, Moses appears as the great prophetic figure. Alongside various phenomena (in particular soothsaying) there developed in Israel a real prophetic tradition which perpetuated itself in the disciples of the prophets.

The prophetic charism is a charism of revelation which makes known to a human being that which he could not discover by his own powers. Its object is both manifold and unique: it is the plan of salvation which will be accomplished and unified in Jesus Christ. 'In many and various ways God spoke of old to our fathers by the prophets; but in these last days he has spoken to us by a son, whom he appointed the heir of all things' (Heb. 1.1–2).

So the New Testament is aware of fulfilling the promises of the Old. Jesus appeared in the midst of a network of prophecy (Zechariah, Simeon, Anna and John the Baptist).

With Pentecost comes the prophecy of Moses: 'Would that all the Lord's people were prophets' (Num. 11.29). The charism of prophecy is frequent in the apostolic church, but like the other charisms it is for the good of the community.

The prophet edifies, exhorts, consoles. However, he always remains under the jurisdiction of the church. Paul asked that everything should be examined with discernment. The prophet cannot exploit his title beyond the function which he exercises in the community and the group to which he attaches himself and which finally judges him.

Prophetic activity did not stop with the apostolic age. It would be difficult to understand the mission of numerous saints, men and women, in the church without reference to the prophetic charisma.

Even today, prophets vitalize Christian communities. Within the church they prompt conversion, they bear witness to the relevance of the beatitudes, they incarnate the absolute character of the call of God for a people of baptized Christians for whom the temptation to be lukewarm is always round the corner. Men and women, by their words and their life they signify the radical character of the message and prompt us to vigilance. But as Jesus of Nazareth said, it is difficult to be a prophet in one's own country!

The prophets Jeremiah and Isaiah. Detail of the mosaics of the Basilica of St Clement, Rome. Twelfth century. Photo private collection.

mistrust any self-justification in relation to scripture detached from its roots when we are ourselves detached from our own roots in the church.

But the prophets are also present in the history of the church. The living tradition is equally based on witnesses who dare to commit themselves in the steps of Christ to the absolute name of God. These figures, humble or famous, still remind us today of God's struggles in human history. The today of the gospel is signified to us in these lives which express the power and credibility of the divine plan.

Moreover the church recognizes that the divine action has continued in the form of certain appearances. The history of the church is marked by supernatural events with which some great saints have been favoured. The church has always considered these visions to belong to the private sphere, and to the degree that such visions and revelations contain nothing contrary to the faith and the tradition of the creed has interpreted them as signs intended to illuminate a vocation, to respond to a more pressing call to conversion and sanctity. However, the church has also recognized and approved the supernatural, divine origin of certain appearances of Mary. In these cases it is not a matter of satisfying a spontaneous need for the miraculous but in a long and difficult process of discernment of affirming the conformity of a message with the whole of revelation. The criterion of truth remains John's affirmation: 'God sent the Son into the world that the world might be saved through him' (John 3.17).

24　I Believe in the Church

When the Niceno-Constantinopolitan creed leads us to say 'I believe in the Church', it is not introducing a fourth proposition complementary to the three propositions relating to the Trinity. Here the Church is the first work of the Spirit whose active presence is confessed in the human heart. The new awareness that the Church has had of itself since Vatican II locates the Church in the mystery of the Trinity which is its source, so that St Cyprian writes; 'The universal Church appears as a people which draws its unity from the Father, the Son and the Holy Spirit.' And Tertullian: 'Since the testimony of the faith and the guarantee of salvation has as its guarantors the three Persons, it is necessary for a mention of the Church to be added, for where there are the three, Father, Son and Holy Spirit, there is also the Church which is the body of the three.'

In the breath of the resurrection

The resurrection of Christ proclaimed in the power of the Holy Spirit manifests the coming into being of the body of Christ. The glorified Christ, like a grain of wheat sown in the ground, bears fruit. For St John, when Jesus has handed over his Spirit to his Father, the blood of sacrifice and the water of life given in abundance flow from his pierced side.

As in a new creation, on the first day the week, John shows us the Risen Christ coming to meet his disciples and to breathe on them: 'Receive the Holy Spirit. If you forgive the sins of any, they are forgiven; if you retain the sins of any, they are retained' (20.23).

This breathing, which will be echoed by the wind of Pentecost, will lead the disciples where they did not want to go. It will make them witnesses to the point of shedding their blood, conforming them to Christ. They will remember that 'He who believes in me will also do the works that I do; and greater works than these will he do, because I go to the Father' (John 14.12). Well before the Gospels were written, the disciples applied themselves to this twofold mission. It is a mission which Jesus of Nazareth entrusted to the disciples he had chosen and a mission welcomed in the breath of the Spirit of the glorified Christ.

The birth of the Church

The Church that we shall see coming to birth in the long narrative of the book of the Acts of the Apostles is not born out of human will but out of God's concern for salvation: it does not come into being in favourable social and religious circumstances, but through the manifestation of the gift of God. It comes to birth in a slow work of gestation to which the Acts of the Apostles bears witness, a patient development in the vicissitudes of history. Far from being a harmonious progress, this birth was marked by oppositions, mutations, persecutions and tensions. Before building the Church, before organizing it, the apostles were to receive it as the mysterious reality of the presence of the Risen Christ in their midst. 'Why do you persecute me' St Paul heard a voice say on the Damascus road when he was persecuting the first Christians.

Thus the Church springs forth from the life of the Trinity. It anchors the mystery of the revela-

Roman fresco of Agnani. Photo private collection

The epiclesis

The epiclesis (from the Greek) is an invocation for the reality of the resurrection to be made real in the community involved in celebration. At the heart of the eucharistic prayer, which forms a whole, an epiclesis is pronounced for the consecration of gifts and another asks for the sanctification of the faithful. Marked by greater attention to the actions of Christ by the person of the priest, the Western tradition concentrated its attention above all on the moment of transubstantiation. It is a fact that the Roman canon does not have any epiclesis to the Holy Spirit. The eucharistic prayers brought into use after Vatican II have given their true place to epicleses.

By his action at the heart of the eucharist, the Holy Spirit allows us to experience the invitation formulated by St Augustine:

'Become what you have received.' What the Spirit has realized in Christ to make him the head he works in us to make us his members, to bring about the sanctification of his body.

tion of the incarnate God in human life. It appears as humanity which welcomes salvation in Jesus Christ. And the welcome of this salvation is seen as a mission, that of announcing the wonders that God accomplishes in the world.

Overwhelmed by the Spirit, the apostles were led from Jerusalem to the ends of the earth. They had the experience of a continual foundation, a continual mutation. The Samaritans and then the Gentiles welcomed the word of God. 'If then God gave the same gift to them as he gave to us when we believed in the Lord Jesus Christ, who was I that I could withstand God?' (Acts .7).

From the beginning the missionary dimension makes up the Church. That is the doing of the work of God who 'desires all men to be saved and to come to the knowledge of the truth' (I Tim. 2.4).

Beyond the tensions

We know the profound mark which this opening up to the Gentiles made on the first Christians. The apostles themselves were divided in a common concern to be faithful to the Lord. So Paul opposed Peter in public when Peter came to Antioch (Gal. 2.11). The topic of the dispute may seem to us today to be somewhat petty, but it must be remembered that it related to a very important question of faith, since it related to the possibility of the Gentiles being able to receive the good news and live it out without conforming to the ancestral disciplines of the Jewish law.

All through history the missionary perspective has often been marked by this opposition between two dynamisms: one, centrifugal, calls the church to advance on a broad front (by espousing new cultures); the other, centripetal, represents the need to consolidate in the name of custom.

One Church, sacrament of the covenant

Because it participates in the life of God, con-stantly receiving his love, the Church becomes the people of God. It is the dwelling place of God with men (Rev. 21.3). It is a manifestation in a significant way, to the end of time, of the covenant concluded in the death of Christ on the cross. It is the permanent realization of this salvation.

The key word used by Vatican II to define the church is also 'sacrament': 'Since the Church, in Christ, is in the nature of sacrament – a sign and instrument, that is, of communion with God and of unity among all men . . .' (*Lumen Gentium*, 1). Under the control of the Spirit, the Church is the sign raised up in the midst of the nations, calling men and women to gather together in Jesus Christ. It cannot think of itself as existing for itself, as the little flock of the righteous, the justified. We are well aware of this permanent temptation through the history of the Church.

This sacramental dimension puts the Church in a situation of continual exodus, of radical poverty. It cannot regard itself as an end in itself. It is called on to follow on the mystery of the incarnation. 'As the assumed nature, insepar-ably united to him, serves the divine Word as a living organ of salvation, so, in a somewhat similar way, does the social structure of the Church serve the Spirit of Christ who vivifies it, in the building up of the body' (*Lumen Gentium*, 8).

The Church, in the power of the Spirit, is called to continual conversions if it is to remain faithful to its Lord. It must ceaselessly ask itself about the witness that it bears by listening to the word of God. The sign of salvation in the midst of humankind, the Church cannot disregard the way in which it is perceived. It cannot spare itself this constant disquiet, since the sign always runs the risk of becoming insignificant, not to mention becoming a sign pointing in the opposite direction. The Church does not exist for itself, just as the Hebrew people was not chosen on its merits. The Church is invited to signify the free gift of God who gives it life and persistance.

A people of forgiven sinners

As a sign of the kingdom in human history, the Church reminds us that God 'willed to make men holy and save them, not as individuals without any bond or link between them, but rather to make them into a people who might acknowledge him and serve him in holiness' (*Lumen Gentium*, 9). So as people of God, body of Christ and temple of the Spirit, the Church is the community of believers gathered by the Spirit. The word *ecclesia*, the ancient Greek word for Church, means both calling and meeting or assembly. As a community of the disciples of Christ, the Church will be marked all down its history by human heaviness. Called to be the spouse adorned for her husband, for some people she sometimes becomes a radical obstacle to an encounter with Jesus Christ.

As the mystical body of Christ, the Church is constructed to the rhythm of human history and bears its scars. We would often like it to be without blemish, totally transparent to the action of the Spirit, and we discover it to be profoundly human.

As the people of God *en route* to the kingdom, the Church must use its pilgrim state as an opportunity. When we look at its history, we should want to be able to strike a mean between the worse and the better and remember only the hours of glory. Believers always gain from not being amnesiacs. It is through an alternation of light and shade that the word of God has come to us. When at Vatican II the bishops reflected on the declaration on religious liberty, a large number of them asked for a chapter of the document to contain this clear re-reading of history . . . Unfortunately the final document bore no trace of it.

The rigorous work of historians in particular has helped us to re-read certain stages in the life of the Church. This is something that has to be done if the tradition is not to become a simple compilation.

25   Baptism and the Gift of the Spirit

Confirmation, 'the sacrament of the Spirit'

Since Christian baptism is a baptism in the Spirit, what does this new sacrament mean? Does it have any specific feature?

Vatican II declares: 'By the sacrament of Confirmation they are more perfectly bound to the Church and are endowed with the special strength of the Holy Spirit' (*Lumen Gentium*, 11).

Confirmation is intended to make the Christian adult. It makes him or her pass from the stage of reception (baptism) to the stage of sharing responsibilities. Without becoming the sacrament of commitment, of militancy, the sacrament of confirmation reinforces membership of the Church in order to bring about sharing in the responsibilities of the community. It makes the faithful capable of receiving ministries. In this way we can understand better why, in the West, confirmation is reserved for the bishop. We can also understand why, pastorally, it is important to confer this sacrament only at an age when the young person is open to a wider reality and comes out of a kind of egocentrism.

The French Conference of Bishops has left some latitude here. While the Church fully reaffirms the priesthood of all the baptized (*Lumen Gentium*, 10ff.), it seems essential to stress the sacrament of confirmation (despite some pastoral ambiguities) as a sacrament of personal commitment in the service of the Church, which takes place in a particular place.

Overwhelmed by Peter's words on the morning of Pentecost, his audience asked him, 'What shall we do?' The apostle's response was clear: 'Repent, and be baptized every one of you in the name of Jesus Christ for the forgiveness of your sins; and you shall receive the Holy Spirit' (Acts 2.37–38). Thus the action of John the Baptist is taken up by the apostles without our being very clear as to whether Jesus himself baptized. John is the only one to mention it, and he does so in a contradictory way (3.22; 4.2). John the Baptist had announced baptism in the Spirit and in fire (Matt. 3.11) and Jesus had said to Nicodemus: 'Unless one is born of water and the Spirit, he cannot see the kingdom of God' (John 3.3). Besides, Matthew and Mark are witnesses to a specific sending on the part of the Risen Christ.

Identification with Christ

Baptized in the Spirit, the disciple is identified with Christ dead and risen. Paul even speaks of burial: 'We were buried therefore with him by baptism into death, so that as Christ was raised from the dead by the glory of the Father, we too might walk in newness of life' (Rom. 6.4).

The Spirit raises up the faithful with Christ by incorporating them into him. Hence the expression 'in Christ' which we find regularly in Paul: 'For as many of you as were baptized in Christ put on Christ' (Gal. 3.27).

The same movement of resurrection comes about where God calls to life by giving his power, his love, his grace. He does this in complete freedom. Thus when the Spirit of God comes upon the Gentiles, Peter declares: 'Can anyone

The Baptism of Christ. Mediaeval manuscript. Photo private collection.

forbid water for baptizing these people who have received the Holy Spirit just as we have' (Acts 10.47). And he orders that Cornelius and his family are to be baptized in the name of Jesus Christ.

Baptism, like faith, introduces the believer into the messianic people which is the vehicle of the Spirit (cf. Gal. 3.14). Because it is an eschatological sign, baptism is only given once. It incorporates into Christ in a very real way. The Christian is made one with Christ. In Christ he can call God Father. He is constituted a child of God in Jesus Christ.

Sanctified by pure grace, the Christian becomes holy as a member of the risen body of Christ. He is as it were brought into the burning bush which burns without being consumed. He radiates love, for from then on 'none of us lives to himself and none of us dies to himself' (Rom. 14.7).

A slow course of conversion

Faith in Christ can come into being in many ways, and the Gospels relate encounters which begin with a badly formulated request or one which expresses a purely physical need. Jesus of Nazareth welcomes these approaches and guides them into a way which expresses desire and confidence: 'If you knew the gift of God . . .' (John 4.10).

Beyond the message, the good news, the encounter with Christ is an encounter with a person. It is a call to conversion: 'Come, follow me.' We give this change of direction, this reversal, the name conversion. Expressed in a radical way in the text, it is the business of a lifetime. It is not just a moment of life but a whole way of living. But how does one live in an attempt to respond to a call without accepting death at the same time: dying to other choices, dying to securities, dying to beliefs. Paul wrote a great deal about dying to the old man to bring the new man to birth.

As a second birth, baptism calls for a way of remaining faithful in the light of Christ. United to Christ's death and resurrection, those who are baptized are raised with Christ: 'Seek the things that are above, where Christ is, seated at the right hand of God. Set your mind on things that are above, not on things that are on earth. For you have died, and your life is hid with Christ in God. When Christ who is our life appears, then you also will appear with him in glory' (Col. 3.1–3).

Baptized to bear witness

Called by Christ, like the apostles, those who are baptized are sent by him into the world and for the world. They participate in the threefold mission of Christ: priest, prophet and king. Over and above difference of responsibility, and taking account of the specific character of the ordained ministries, all those who have been baptized participate in a common priesthood which roots them in the desire of God. In the gift of the Spirit, each one is called to bear witness and give an account 'of the hope that is in him'. Faith is this treasure which the Church carries in earthen vessels and which commits the community of believers.

'The whole body of the faithful who have an anointing that comes from the holy one cannot err in matters of belief. This characteristic is shown in the supernatural appreciation of the faith of the whole people, when, "from the bishops to the last of the faithful", they manifest a universal consent in matters of faith and morals. By this appreciation of the faith, aroused and sustained by the Spirit of truth, the People of God, guided by the sacred teaching authority, and obeying it, receives not the mere word of men, but truly the word of God, the faith once for all delivered to the saints. The People unfailingly adheres to this faith, penetrates it more deeply with right judgment, and applies it more fully in daily life' (*Lumen Gentium*, 12).

This witness to the faith is expressed in words, the affirmation of convictions, but it is primarily realized in the specific and everyday commitment of all who are baptized. This presence in the world was stressed at the Second Vatican Council. The Christian must not run away from the contingent to take refuge in a supposedly spiritual world sheltered from the ups and downs of this world. The presence of the baptized must be active and not passive, and certainly not fearful. As the yeast leavens the loaf, the pains and labours of this life are not occasions for gaining heaven but participation in a project under the direction of the Holy Spirit.

A diversity of spiritual gifts

The Holy Spirit received in the sacrament of baptism is manifested in every sacrament. The sacramental life irrigates Christian existences. The Spirit makes our talents flower, and it makes our deserts flower as well. How can not one stress the humour of the Holy Spirit who is able to use our weaknesses and our faults in this way? It is a tricky task to interpret the presence of the Spirit, since he does not blow only where we want. He is unexpected and never ceases to surprise us. He remains God's surprise and does not allow us to rest on our achievements.

The flourishing of the particular gifts which scripture calls 'charisms' is one of the fruits of the Spirit. In the letter to the Corinthians St Paul rejoices when they spring up, but he sees that

133

they also need to be regulated. In fact, if they are gifts of God, the charisms must serve to contribute to the vitality of the body of Christ. They are not an end in themselves. The Spirit communicates himself for the good of all. The diversity of gifts must serve the common good. Conversely, the only communion which can flourish in the Church is that which respects and promotes diversity. Recognition and encouragement of the other remains the condition for the existence of the body *qua* body: 'If all were a single organ, where would the body be?' (I Cor. 12.19). These gifts are manifold, and the lists which St Paul gives of them are neither systematic nor exhaustive. A Church which tended towards uniformity would risk either atrophy or explosion since it would quench the Spirit who brings unity in diversity. But having stressed this diversity, Paul adds: 'But earnestly desire the higher gifts. And I will show you a still more excellent way . . . If I have not love I am nothing' (12.31; 13.2).

Charisms and institution

So it would seem difficult to contrast a Church based on a free abundance of spiritual gifts with a more institutional Church. The reciprocal relationship will allow only the Church to recognize itself in the power of the Spirit of Christ. There is a temptation to lay great stress on the spiritual gifts when the weight of the institution seems to put a brake on evangelization. Thus there are those who could contrast a spiritual dynamic with a more institutional dynamic. The Church has a specific responsibility in the discernment of spiritual gifts, but law must not quench life. To avoid any subjectivism, the interpretation of a charism can only take place in the Church in conjunction with those who exercise a ministerial charism in the Church. 'We beseech you, brethren, to respect those who labour among you and are over you in the Lord and admonish you, and to esteem them very highly in love because of their work' (I Thess. 5.12).

Renewal in the Spirit

When Pope John XXIII called for a New Pentecost for the Church, he certainly did not envisage the vast evangelical growth that we have been experiencing over the last twenty years.

The renewal is first of all a spiritual experience: the experience of a profound freedom in prayer, an immediate relationship to God, a joy and peace which are felt and communicated.

Without denying anything of the sacramental life (quite the contrary), the renewal gives or restores the taste of thanksgiving, of praise.

The spiritual experience is that of the community (prayer meeting) and is an invitation to communication, to sharing, to witness.

Beyond the rigours of a world dominated by a general climate of rationalism and organization, the renewal stresses a certain childlikeness in which feelings regain their place. It restores a place to charisms (tangible manifestations of the presence of the Spirit) which every person possesses and which must, with discernment, be put at the service of the edification of the church.

The renewal is a living sign that the promises of the New Testament are not solely behind us. God today is very present in history and people live only by the gift of his grace.

We should also mistrust too great a stress on immediacy (in the relationship to the Word, to God, to the other), immediacy which suppresses history and the incarnate reality of humanity, immediacy which can express a psychological need more than a spiritual quest.

Emotionally intense awareness of the intervention of God is not a criterion of the truth of the presence of the Spirit. Finally, if God acts directly towards humanity and in it, it is never without human co-operation or beside human co-operation. The direct action of God always manifests itself through the medium of history or society.

26 The Spirit Manifests the Sin of the World

When Jesus promises the Holy Spirit to his disciples, he tells them: 'And when he comes, he will convince the world of sin and of righteousness and of judgment' (John 16.8). If the Spirit comes to make real the gift of God, the Father's faithfulness to his plan of love, he must inevitably bring to light whatever is opposed to this plan, this covenant. The power of the Spirit, the power of communion, illuminates with the light of a new day all that amounts to a rejection of God in the human heart.

God's faithfulness to his covenant

The prophets who spoke in the name of God had already denounced the hardness of heart and the stubborn necks of the children of Israel. They did not cease to invite the Jewish people to conversion. Jeremiah had prophesied the perspective of a new covenant. God promised to give men a new heart by the action of his Spirit and he would forgive sin: 'I will pardon their transgression and their sin I will remember no more' (Jer. 31.34). Over and above the transgressions of his people, God does not cease to restate his plan of love. He does not go back on his word.

Now the sinner is the person who shuts himself or herself off from the word of God, from his grace. In this way he or she enters the spiral of self-justification and refuses to be responsible before God.

When he sees Jesus coming to meet him, John the Baptist says, 'Behold the lamb of God who takes away the sin of the world' (John 1.29). This description must certainly be seen as a link between the Suffering Servant of Isaiah ('Like a lamb that is led to the slaughter . . . he was killed', Isa. 53.7–8), and the rite of the paschal lamb, a symbol of the redemption of Israel. In welcoming salvation the believer believes himself to be directly and personally involved with this lamb of God. The saving mystery of the cross calls for our conversion, the recognition of our unworthiness: 'Lord, I am not worthy, but say only one word and I shall be healed.' The expression of the justice and the love of God which is realized on the cross reveals to those who commit their life to following Christ the truth and the depth of their sin: it also reveals to them their own involvement in the sin of the world.

Bearing witness to reconciliation

The revelation of forgiveness allows us to grasp the reality and the depth of sin. The lifegiving Spirit illuminates in a new way the death which is at work in each one of our lives. This slow process of giving birth goes on and the church has the responsibility to keep alive this ministry (service) of reconciliation: 'We beseech you on behalf of Christ, be reconciled to God. For our sake he made him to be sin who knew no sin, that in him we might become the righteousness of God' (II Cor. 5.20–21).

Christ came, scripture tells us, to save that which was lost. He denounces sin and reveals at the same stroke the Father's mercy for the sinner. At the risk of scandalizing those who witness such mercy, he presents the good news of forgiveness in words and actions.

Over and above this human sin, Christ denounces and brings to light the sin of the world. The Son of God triumphs over this power of darkness which rejects the light. In his own way John tells us that Jesus has overcome the world (John 16.33). The disobedience of the first man introduced sin into the human race; the obedience of the firstborn of all creation introduces humanity to the abundance of grace.

For the remission of sins

From the beginning, Christian baptism has been seen as the crucible of the remission of sins. The fire of the Spirit brings about all sorts of new things in us. But this presence of the Spirit comes up against resistance and opposition in our lives. This struggle is part of the everyday experience of Christians. As Paul describes it, this fight will be one between the flesh and the Spirit: 'Walk by the Spirit, and do not gratify the desires of the flesh. For the desires of the flesh are

Jesus healing the paralysed man. Wood engraving. Photo F. Garnier

against the Spirit, and the desires of the Spirit are against the flesh; for these are opposed to each other, to prevent you from doing what you would' (Gal. 5.16–17). The flesh here denotes the condition of the creature marked by sin and death; this creature is itself called on to participate in the resurrection since 'the Spirit comes to the aid of our weakness' (Rom. 8.26). 'The inner man is strengthened and introduced into a new life, into the supernatural reality of the divine life. Only this slow and continual process of giving birth can lead the Christian to recognize that he or she is truly called to freedom' (Gal. 5.13).

Denouncing sin

In the power of the Spirit the Christian who commits his or her life to following Christ cannot remain indifferent to all that spoils creation. As in a trial, he bears witness to the successes and failures of a Christ who conquers evil. Thus before becoming committed to the faith of the church, the believer is invited to renounce the hold and to reject Satan who is the author of sin.

Renouncing sin for oneself is a hard struggle which only the grace of the sacrament of reconciliation can make humanly possible. In solidarity with the sin of the world the Christian is called on to name sin, to denote it so as to fight it the better. This sin is in the human heart, but it is also in structures. The Pastoral Constitution on the Church in the Modern World, *Gaudium et Spes*, makes this quite specific: 'all offences against life itself, such as murder, genocide, abortion, euthanasia and wilful suicide; all violations of the integrity of the human person, such as mutilation, physical and mental torture, undue psychological pressures; all offences against human dignity, such as subhuman living conditions, arbitrary imprisonment, deportation, slavery, prostitution, the selling of women and children, degrading working conditions where men are treated as mere tools for profit rather than as free and responsible persons' (27).

The sin against the Spirit

'And every one who speaks a word against the Son of man will be forgiven; but he who blasphemes against the Holy Spirit will not be forgiven' (Luke 12.10).

What is this sin against the Spirit which is not forgiven? Beyond question it is being radically closed to forgiveness. The word of reconciliation pronounced in Jesus Christ does not reach the person who shuts himself or herself up or is imprisoned in his or her actions. Behind this last possibility, is it not the whole task of the Church which is at stake: showing the world the forgiveness which God offers everyone? There is an urgent mission to keep open room for mercy.

27 One, Holy, Catholic and Apostolic

At the head of the world, to make present the mystery of the Father, the Church, rooted in the words of the Son, bears witness to the power of the Spirit. It grows out of the life of the Trinity. It is the earthly reflection of the communion of the three Persons. The spirit of communion, the Holy Spirit is given for the life of the body of Christ. St Paul reminds us that we have 'all been baptized in one Spirit to form one body' (I Cor. 12.13).

Where is the Church?

This unique body of Christ has been given expression in various forms over the course of history. The mystical body is a visible body, a historical body. Moreover when we talk of the Church we cannot limit ourselves to what it is in the desire of God. In this bond between visible reality and invisible nature, the signs of the authenticity of the Church have been expressed since the Council of Constantinople by the four dimensions 'one', 'holy', 'catholic' and 'apostolic'.

In the face of heresies, these four 'marks' have become apologetic arguments. But we should not forget that they have force only with reference to the gospel. It is impossible to make them values in themselves. They remain tasks, a summons to put ourselves at the disposal of the dynamic of the Spirit.

Unity to be achieved

In the body, the Spirit is a principle of unity. It realizes the prayer of Christ, 'That they may all be one, even as thou, Father, art in me, and I in thee, that they may also be in us, so that the world may believe that thou hast sent me' (John 17.21). The Church proceeds from the unity of the event of salvation and the unity of the message. The many constitute a single body in Christ, and the apostle Paul puts the Christians of Corinth on guard against the temptation to put themselves under other authorities (cf. I Cor. 10.10–30). The texts contain numerous exhortations to believers to fight against fragmentations, against divisions. Given human diversity, human sensibilities, options, cultures and historical situations, unity cannot be the fruit of a concensus. The Church cannot be reduced to the sum total of the individuals who form it. This given unity must constantly be produced. The Letter to the Ephesians gives us a profound reason for this demand: 'I therefore, a prisoner for the Lord, beg you to lead a life worthy of the calling to which you have been called, with all lowliness and meekness, with patience, forbearing one another in love, eager to maintain the unity of the Spirit in the bond of peace. There is one body and one Spirit, just as you were called to the one hope that belongs to your call, one Lord, one faith, one baptism, one God and Father of us all, who is above all and through all and in all' (Eph. 3.16).

Unity in respect of the differences

The Church has to live out this unity while respecting diversity. The Council reminds us that it is a communion of local churches. Thus in the New Testament the word *ecclesia* is used in the plural; it is connected with the names of local churches which can sometimes signify different worlds: Jerusalem and Corinth, Antioch and Rome . . . The one Church is fully manifested in each church: the Church of Christ is not a Church made uniform by a process of centralization: it is not egalitarian nor totalitarian. It does not know a joyless uniformity which lacks freedom.

The Church cannot be satisfied with its historical divisions. Vatican II reminds us that 'this division openly contradicts the will of Christ, scandalizes the world and damages that most holy cause, the preaching of the Gospel to every creature' (*Decree on Ecumenism*, 1). It also tells us that our separated brethren rightly bear the name of Christians, and the children of the Catholic Church recognize them fully as brothers and sisters in the Lord.

The course of ecumenism has been marked by significant stages during the twentieth century. We must rejoice at this and at the same time assess what still has to be done. Beyond making symbolic gestures and engaging in common theological quests, the churches must allow themselves to be challenged by the negative witness which their divisions give to the world.

The ministry of unity

Unity in the Church is manifested in communion in the same faith. It is also expressed in communion between the churches, and the collection which Paul organized has been testimony to this since apostolic times. One question remains difficult, that of the ministry of Peter. The differences here are in fact specifically over the interpretation of the affirmation that we find in Matthew: 'You are Peter, and on this rock I will build my Church, and the powers of death shall not prevail against it. I will give you the keys of the kingdom of heaven, and whatever you loose on earth shall be loosed in heaven' (16.18–19). This ministry of communion for the universal Church developed on the Bishop of Rome is the primacy of service and unity in faith. We think it necessary to the structure of the Church, in union with the college of bishops who are concerned for the universal Church. This ministry must remain a power leading to initiatives, suggestions and support for all the churches in the face of the challenges of the present world or the pressure of certain forces.

Unity in holiness

The unity of the Church does not have its source in itself but in the holiness of the God who sends it on its mission in the heart of the world. The holiness of the Church is no more in evidence than its unity. It is in the eyes of faith that the Church is indefectibly holy. The Church is not holy by virtue of those who compose it; they are not better than others. It is the Church that God unceasingly sanctifies. It is both holy and called on to purify itself by living from the Father's forgiveness. Because it is made up of men and women who are both sinners and justified, the Church is the place of permanent struggle between the Spirit of God and evil. Some people have periodically wanted to see it as that citadel of the just who look down on the world where sin abounds. The Church can only pray to God each day for sanctification and holiness, confident in the hope that they will be realized to the degree and in the way that God decides. We should listen to St Augustine on this point: 'Wherever in my books I have described the Church as being without spot or wrinkle, that should not be understood as indicating that that is what the Church already is, but it is preparing to be what it will be when it too appears in glory. For at present, by reasons of the inexperience and all the weaknesses of its members, it must repeat each day the prayer 'Forgive us our sins . . .'

A Church in the process of conversion

The Church is the place where sin is recognized and confessed with a view to forgiveness. The people of God is the messianic people, the people whom God sanctifies to be 'a sign raised up in the midst of the nations'. All those who are baptized are called to sanctity in allowing the Spirit of God to work in them. Because they are all called to the same sanctity, the members of the Church are all equal before God.

The Church is the sacrament of salvation by virtue of the call to conversion which it addresses to all men and women, the means it offers them of bringing about this conversion, and also by its own continual conversion. How can it not be aware of everything today that still disfigures this perception of its holiness? It is by living constantly with a view to conversion that the Church signifies that it receives its holiness only from God. At the same time it must recognize that it is a living paradox. It is a spouse, certainly, but not a spouse without stain; it is more like 'a prostitute whom Christ remarried every day', as the fathers say. In spite of all its wounds, the Church remains a holy Church, set apart to bear witness to the 'today' of salvation. In the midst of the world it remains this communion of saints, a sign that all is grace.

Universal dimensions

One and holy in the desire of God, the Church in the power of the Spirit has to enter into communion with the world. The book of Acts shows us how the Church progresses from Jerusalem to Rome. And yet in the New Testament it is not described as being catholic. It is Ignatius of Antioch (around 110) who uses this term for the first time: 'Where the Bishop shows himself, the people must also be, just as where Jesus Christ is, there is the catholic Church.' He did not invent anything, and located the catholicity of the Church in Jesus Christ. Because he is the fullness of revelation, Christ is recognized as the head of the body which is the Church, and God 'through him has reconciled to himself all things, whether on earth or in heaven, making peace by the blood of the cross' (Col. 1.20).

At the sources of catholicity

So the catholicity of the Church is not tied to its spatial extension. From Jerusalem on, the Church has been catholic. Nor is the Church's catholicity tied to a sociological conception or to its historical continuity.

Catholicity constantly sends the Church back to its profound identity, its foundation in Christ. It is that spiritual dynamic which moves towards Christ (the Way, the Truth and the Life) becoming all in all, the one who by his Spirit gives each generation the words for confessing him Christ and Lord. The Spirit participates in the royal power of Christ according to his earthly condition. By the Holy Spirit, catholicity assumes particular features without destroying them. Moreover, nothing is less catholic in depth than a certain apostolic haste, a clericalism, albeit an innocent one, a narrow confessionalism, a spirit of triumphalism, and finally the paternalist desire to regiment everything, to make everything uniform.

It is true that in the course of history the designation catholic has been used in polemical ways. The Orthodox Church was catholic in opposing all heresies. The Reformation raised the question as to the right of using the term. This produced a shift in its significance, and only the Roman Church has kept it. The link between the word 'catholic' and this one church is so strong that several Protestant churches have given it up in irritation or resignation. In the creed 'catholic' has sometimes been replaced

The Last Supper. Detail. Thirteenth century. Sardinia. Photo private collection.

with 'universal' to avoid confusion. It is no longer possible, as people thought at one time, to refuse all catholicity to the great communions separated from the Roman Church. A clear understanding of catholicity leads us to a better understanding of mission as a perspective of the encounter between every person (and every culture) and the salvation offered in Jesus Christ. Moreover, 'if the Church is to be in a position to offer all men and women the mystery of salvation and the life brought by God, then it must implant itself among all these groups in the same way that Christ by his incarnation committed himself to the particular social and cultural circumstances of the men among whom he lived' (*Decree on the Church's Missionary Activity*, 10).

The apostolicity of the Church

We have considered the unity, the holiness and the catholicity of the Church. It can be asked when and to what degree we have in the Church something that is one, holy and catholic. The fourth mark of the Church expressively gives a decisive criterion: the Church is only truly one, holy and catholic when it is apostolic. 'We are witness to these things, we and the Holy Spirit whom God has given to those who obey him' (Acts 5.32), Peter tells the Sanhedrin. The apostles are witnesses by affirming the will and commitment of God realized in his covenant on the cross. The witness attests what has happened by an active expectation of the return of the Saviour. So the apostolicity of the Church is the guarantee of its fidelity in the Spirit to the mission entrusted to it.

A Church founded on the apostles

Very soon the Church was to recognize that certain witnesses had a special place and a special responsibility. But who are the apostles? Certainly there is the group of twelve chosen by Jesus of Nazareth, who several times were given an explicit mission. There is also Matthias, who was added to the Twelve after the Ascension. 'So one of the men who have accompanied us during all the time that the Lord Jesus went in and out amongst us, beginning from the baptism of John until the day when he was taken up from us, one of these men must become with us a witness to his resurrection' (Acts 1.21,22). But there is also Paul, who does not hesitate to present himself as an apostle (Rom. 1.1), and those whom he describes as apostles with relative freedom.

By preaching the gospel the apostle evokes faith and brings together the community of believers. By reason of his message, at the same time he has full power to found and govern churches. In this sense the Church is the edifice whose foundation is the apostles and whose cornerstone is Jesus Christ.

The apostolic succession

This apostolic tradition is handed down in

The Apostles Paul, Peter and Andrew.
Detail. Romanesque sculpture from the cloister of the abbey of Santo Domingo de Silos, Spain.
Photo private collection

inspired scripture. The catholic Church recognizes and confesses that this apostolic tradition continues in the apostolic succession. 'The bishops also have been designated by the Holy Spirit to take the place of the apostles as pastors of souls and, together with the Supreme Pontiff and subject to his authority, they are commissioned to perpetuate the work of Christ, the eternal Pastor' (*Decree on the Pastoral Office of Bishops in the Church*, 2).

Of course an individual bishop does not succeed an individual apostle (except in the case of the Bishop of Rome). The succession is a succession from college to college, from a stable and structured group to a constituted group. The apostolic succession works through consecration and the laying on of hands. But it is also formed by the conservation of doctrine handed down since the time of the apostles. So the Pastoral Epistles speak of safeguarding the transmission of true doctrine. We must also recognize that the whole Church is apostolic, since all the faithful keep the sacred deposit of the word of God in such a way that 'in maintaining, practising and professing the faith that has been handed down there should be a remarkable harmony between the bishops and the faithful' (*Constitution on Revelation*, 10). Trusting in the promise of its Lord ('Behold, I am with you to the end of the world'), the Church recognizes that the treasure of revelation has been entrusted to it. The witness of the gospel cannot keep silent. He or she speaks with sincerity, from God, in the face of God, in Christ (cf. II Cor. 2.17).

All the holy people of God participate in the prophetic function of Christ. On the basis of the apostolic experience, the Church always lives in the newness of the encounter with its risen Lord in the Spirit.

28   A Faith Marked by Expectation

Why do we have to wait until 'all is fulfilled' (John 19.30)? If it is true that Jesus Christ is the full revelation of God, is it not enough to live our daily lives in faithfulness to his message, his life and his death? The Christian faith could only be a more or less dynamizing remembrance. We could choose to live out our lives in reference to the good news, as one philosophy among others.

In its trinitarian structure the creed invites us to enter into the offer of a covenant. The Spirit which is given us opens our hearts to hope. The resurrection of Jesus and his exaltation to the right hand of the Father inaugurate the 'already there' of the promised kingdom, yet the gospel stresses the need to 'watch', to 'abide'. These two verbs indicate the sphere of expectation, the place of a hoped-for return.

The return of the Lord

The first Church experienced this expectation of the parousia, the progressively postponed horizon of which was the return of the Lord. 'The Spirit and the bride say, "Come" ' (Rev. 22.17). Easter has inaugurated the time of the realization of the promises. This first day of the week opens the time of a new creation which is in process of giving birth. The resurrection is at work. It does not lead the believer to flee his creaturely condition in dreaming and enthusiasm: it gives him or her a historical responsibility which is attested by all the texts which speak of judgment. 'When Christ who is our life appears, then you also will appear with him in glory' (Col. 3.4).

Intent on the realization of the promises, the Christian hopes for the coming of the kingdom of peace and joy in the Spirit. Christ is this kingdom in person, and our participation in his life opens up to us the perspective of a full and complete participation in his resurrection: 'See what love the Father has given us, that we should be called children of God, and so we are. The reason why the world does not know us is that it did not know him. Beloved, we are God's children now; it does not yet appear what we shall be, but we know that when he appears we shall be like him, for we shall see him as he is' (I John 3.1–2).

An existence in tension

We have the firstfruits, the pledges of the Spirit. All Christian experience lies in this tension between 'now already' and 'not yet'. St Paul also reminds us: 'We who have the firstfruits of the Spirit, groan inwardly as we wait for adoption as sons, the redemption of our bodies. For in this hope we are saved' (Rom. 8.23).

The Spirit which raised up Jesus of Nazareth will give life to our mortal bodies in the same way. 'I am the resurrection. He who believes in me, though he die, yet shall he live, and whoever lives and believes in me shall never die' (John 11.25–26). What is expressed in terms of kingdom or reign of God in the Synoptic Gospels and in St Paul is expressed in terms of life in St John. 'I came that they may have life, and have it abundantly' (John 10.10). The work of the Spirit achieves its fullness of truth only in the perspective of a participation in the inheritance of our divine sonship. The images used to speak of this encounter differ, and the Gospel parables which refer to it stress a twofold aspect: the complete freedom in which the invitation is offered and the conversion needed to prove worthy of it (cf. Matt. 22.1–4).

Christian existence, then, unfolds between the 'already there' of the kingdom experienced in the resurrection of Christ made present in sacramental life and the 'not yet' of this kingdom of peace and power in the Spirit. This existence in tension is sometimes difficult to take. There is a temptation to overstress one aspect to the detriment of the other. It is the articulation of the two which opens up hope. Hope is not a dream, it is the future as open to the name of God's plan of love.

The advent of the kingdom

Leaving behind the idea of a closed destiny inscribed in the stars or elsewhere, the Christian goes forward with trust in the one who is the embodiment of justice. The advent of the kingdom has always stirred the imagination. Some people have made calculations to work out how near it is, forgetting what Jesus said: 'Heaven and earth will pass away, but my words will not pass away. But of that day or that hour no one knows, not even the angels in heaven, nor the Son, but only the Father' (Mark 13.31–32). Others paint impressive pictures containing details of the last judgment. Let us rescue the faith of these believers from excesses of imagination! Even the efforts of St Paul in I Corinthians

15 to describe in more detail how the dead are raised leave us unsatisfied. Do we have no image to feed our imagination of that which gives us life and hope? The image of the grain of wheat which dies invites us to think of the harvest. Granted, it does not tell us enough about the freedom of the divine initiative. The Church is a sacrament of this kingdom. It cannot identify it with an element in its historical future. It points towards it and makes it present in a mysterious way by welcoming the gift of God. Intent on the realization of this kingdom, the disciples of Jesus Christ have the active desire to make all men and women children of God by gathering together in unity the dispersed children of God to make a single people, a people which hymns the wonders of the Father.

To say that the Church is a sign of salvation in the midst of humankind ensures that it is not confused with the world and at the same time that it is not the realization of the kingdom. It must not be confused with the world, otherwise it would no longer be a sign of anything, and at the same time it is not outside or over against the world, otherwise the sign that it gives could no longer be perceived. It must not be confused with the fulfilment of the kingdom and must constantly be open to other cultures. It has never finished going to the ends of the earth and discovering how the Spirit has already preceded it in human hearts.

29 Resurrection of the Dead, Resurrection of the Flesh

'Christ is risen.' This affirmation expresses the essentials of the Christian faith. In a sense the resurrection of Jesus is the one Christian truth: 'If you confess with your lips that Jesus is Lord and believe in your heart that God raised him from the dead, you will be saved' (Rom. 10.9).

But this unique event only assumes its total dimension in our resurrection. Let us remember Paul's argument: 'If there is no resurrection of the dead, then Christ has not been raised' (I Cor. 15.13). Christ is the firstfruits. The first sheaf of the harvest has been garnered and consecrated to God: the whole harvest will follow. Life in Christ has already begun. Moreover that is the reason why the Christian does not believe in reincarnation. The resurrection to which Christ introduces us at the time of our baptism is not the survival of the spiritual part of us which escapes the dissolution of matter, but a recreation in glory.

The truth of the incarnation

Whereas the Nicene Creed speaks of the resurrection of the dead, the Apostles' Creed invites us to believe in the resurrection of the flesh, the body. Without attempting to imagine this resurrection and allowing it its radical newness ('Behold, I make all things new', Rev. 21.5), we can say something more about why the Christian hope is focussed on the resurrection of the flesh.

Let us remember Job: 'I know that my redeemer lives, and at last he will stand upon the earth; and after my skin has been destroyed, then from my flesh I shall see God, whom I shall see on my side, and my eyes shall behold, and

not another. My heart faints within me' (Job 19.25–27). The flesh is this reality created by God which gives me roots in a human history. It is this complex of relationships, this person that I am and in whom God comes by his spirit to make his home if I am willing to receive him. Far from being an accident (a prison, as in Plato), the flesh is that by which our existence has a value. The Word was made flesh and invites us to take our bodily human condition seriously.

A body for glory

St Paul recalled: 'Do you not know that your body is a temple of the Holy Spirit within you, which you have from God? You are not your own' (I Cor. 6.19).

In Christianity the body is called to holiness, called to participate fully in the glory of God. It is in his flesh that Christ has saved us. His crucified flesh is glorified. At no moment in the memory of the apostles does the resurrection come to *erase* the experience of the cross. The resurrection of the flesh manifests the importance that all human life has for God and justifies the Church's fight for the dignity of all human life. Death is not the ultimate end of the body, since it is not the ultimate human experience. In the name of the resurrection of Jesus Christ we believe in the commitment of God to human history. God willed to revive in him that manner of living which is expressed in the incarnation. To the degree that we live by the Holy Spirit poured out on all flesh we presuppose that God will do for us precisely what he has already done for his Son.

It is easy for us to neglect this perspective of

The Resurrection of the Dead. Portal of the Last Judgment. Bourges Cathedral. Photo Remi Tournus

our act of faith, since it upsets the way in which we understand death and our own body. Our society has put particular stress on the body and at the same time has disguised death. Immersion in the waters of baptism (which is demonstrated well in baptism by immersion) calls on us to welcome salvation in the totality of our existence. Risen with Christ, we bear witness from now on to a life given in abundance which in the will of God is destined to blossom into eternal life.

Having mentioned the Church in which we live spiritually, the Apostles' Creed adds three major experiences: communion or solidarity among the disciples of Christ, the forgiveness of sins and finally the hope, in a world to come, of resurrection and eternal life. These experiences are closely bound up with one another. At the heart of the faith the resurrection signifies the truth of our return to the Father. He who is the origin of all things is also the one towards whom we are going. As we are caught up in the movement of the Trinity, the act of faith leads us from the Father to the Father, thus recapitulating the self-revelation of God.

30   Do not Quench the Spirit

This warning of Paul to the Christians of Thessalonica and those in authority among them must not be forgotten. Caught up in a new birth, the baptized person opens his or her eyes and has the experience of freedom. It is often difficult to live out this freedom. It is so much easier to resign one's human responsibility. 'Where the spirit of the Lord is, there is freedom. And we all, with unveiled face, beholding the glory of the Lord, are being changed into his likeness from one degree of glory to another, for this comes from the Lord who is the Spirit' (II Cor. 3.17–18). We find it easier to enter into a logic of imprisonment than into a logic of giving birth.

If we cannot invent the faith, we can reflect on it, and indeed we have to do that, for we can only hand on the faith that we have assimilated. The cosmos and history are the places where we encounter God, and today we are threatened with the danger of sheer spiritualism (bound up with sheer individualism). We forget that 'the creation waits with eager longing for the revealing of the sons of God' (Rom. 8.19).

Taking a breath makes room for the possibility of a word. It gives words their force and their impact. What would happen to an act of faith which became sheer repetition? The treasure that we bear in earthen vessels is a living one. The tradition of the Church is itself alive. Tradition is not just a memory but involves permanently going deeper in the Spirit. In biblical terms we would say that it is also in the heart. It is not just faithful memory, but a living commitment which is ceaselessly renewed.

The apostolic testimony has been given once for all. It is a point of reference. One can only build on its foundation. In this sense Catholic theology says that revelation was closed with the death of the last Apostle.

The tradition is living because it is not a reality external to living spirits given life by the Spirit. It is the gospel written on our hearts. The believer receives it from the Church and his or her brothers and sisters in the faith. This incessant communication of witness given to Jesus Christ in the Spirit constitutes the breeding ground of the Church. This necessary sharing in the faith must not be confused with individual religious sentiment. We speak too easily of our faith as if it were a conviction that we did or did not want to share with other believers.

The creed reminds us that the faith is always the faith of the Church. The liturgy invites us to turn to God, saying to him, 'Look not on our sins but on the faith of your Church.' It is in welcoming the faith of the Church that the baptized person becomes a believer. Each individual is then called to recognize that he or she cannot come before God without establishing a link with others. Faith does not cease to be a grace, but historically it comes about in the solidarity of the Church. The creed also has a highly symbolic function. At the very moment when it is proclaimed it brings about the bond which it sustains.

At the same time we cannot recite the creed without causing it to have further effects within the life of the Church. As the sign of communion, it has its place in the communion of a Church which, as we have said, cannot exist without diversity.

The creed of the Church calls for professions of faith and these have relevance only in a constant dialogue with the symbol of faith. This symbol that we have just studied tells us constantly that in the Spirit and with our brothers and sisters we call God Father in Jesus Christ. Professing the faith of the Church, the baptized person professes the salvation that God offers to all men and women.

The creed is the Church's treasure; but the moment it is proclaimed it gives the Church a task: to bear witness to the glory of God and the salvation of the world.

Christ and the Apostles. Detail of the ancient church of St Saviour in Chora which has now become a mosque. Kahriye Djami. Fourteenth century, Istanbul. Photo Lessing-Magnum

Prayer to the Holy Spirit

Come Holy Ghost, our souls inspire,
And lighten with celestial fire;
Thou the anointing spirit art,
Who dost thy sevenfold gifts impart:

Thy blessed unction from above
Is comfort, life, and fire of love;
Enable with perpetual light
The dullness of our blinded sight:

Anoint and cheer our soiled face
With the abundance of thy grace:
Keep far our foes, give peace at home;
Where thou art guide no ill can come.

Teach us to know the Father, Son,
And thee, of both, to be but one;
That through the ages all along
This may be our endless song,
Praise to thy eternal merit,
Father, Son and Holy Spirit.

J. Cosin (1594–1672)

Based on the ninth-century prayer, *Veni, Creator Spiritus*

Hymn

Come, thou Holy Paraclete,
And from thy celestial seat
Send thy light and brilliancy:
Father of the poor, draw near;
Giver of all gifts, be here;
Come, the soul's true radiancy:

Come, of comforters the best,
Of the soul the sweetest guest,
Come in toil refreshingly:
Thou in labour rest most sweet,
Thou art shadow from the heat,
Comfort in adversity.

O thou Light, most pure and blest,
Shine within the inmost breast
Of thy faithful company.
Where thou are not, man hath nought;
Every holy deed and thought
Comes from thy divinity.

What is soiled, make thou pure;
What is wounded, work its cure;
What is parched, fructify;
What is rigid, gently bend;
What is frozen, warmly tend;
Straighten what goes erringly.

Fill thy faithful, who confide
In thy power to guard and guide,
With thy sevenfold mystery.
Here thy grace and virtue send:
Grant salvation in the end,
And in heaven felicity.

Translation by J. M. Neale of the thirteenth-century hymn, *Veni, sancte Spiritus*